TIMELESS WRITINGS 65

TATAY JOBO ELIZES

PUB. 2023

Published by Tatay Jobo Elizes,
Self-Publisher - 2023

This book is published and printed with a collection of articles obtained from cyberspace, mostly facebook, which are shared publicly as explicitly posted & declared by authors, readers and sharers. The purpose is to make these articles and essays available to the public and promote reading among Filipinos & others, young and old. Printing of this book is using the present day method of Print-On-Demand (POD) system, where prints will never run out of copies.

KDP ISBN – **9798869934017**
Independently published

Anybody is free to copy this book and share with others.

Disclaimer: Views are expressed by the authors alone. Tatay Jobo Elizes does not knowingly publish false information and may not be held liable for the views of the authors exercising their right to free expression.

Self-Publisher's Details:
Contact: job_elizes@yahoo.com +
amazon site: Browse Tatay Jobo Elizes in Books +
my site: www.tatayjoboeiizes.webs.com +
https://www.facebook.com/groups/399368500835109 +
free reading of my published books + other bestsellers

Cover pic: Lady Reader (poster-credits)

. . . .

Contents

....

1
ARCHDIOCESE OF LINGAYEN-DAGUPAN STATEMENT ON THE ENTRY OF OFFICIALS OF THE INTERNATIONAL CRIMINAL COURT INTO THE PHILIPPINES

ARCHDIOCESE
OF
LINGAYEN-DAGUPAN

**STATEMENT ON THE ENTRY OF OFFICIALS OF
THE INTERNATIONAL CRIMINAL COURT
INTO THE PHILIPPINES**

The Church always strives after and cherishes the truth. She proclaims her faith, after all, that saving Truth was made Incarnate in the Man from Nazareth, executed because he dared proclaim the truth to those who preferred the shadow of untruth and ignorance.

It is our understanding that the Prosecutor of the International Criminal Court with its seat at The Hague has sought ingress into the country to pursue inquiry and investigation into the deaths and extrajudicial executions that occurred at the height of the past Administration's "war on drugs".

Insofar as this process seeks to ferret out the truth and, possibly, to hold accountable those who, in an arrogant abuse of power, may have caused others, even possibly innocent people, loss of life in violation of guarantees enshrined in the Philippine Constitution as well as in human rights treaties to which the Philippines is a party, a thorough inquiry by persons without vested interests or prior alliances should be welcome. Truth has never destroyed a nation. It is falsehood that has been the undoing of many peoples.

We understand the concerns that have been voiced about what may appear to be a transgression of Philippine sovereignty. However, allowing the investigators and factfinders in can and should be an act of sovereignty – a choice we, as a people, freely make for the sake of truth and to vindicate those who may have lost their lives, denied by processes of law that every democracy guarantees both to citizen and foreigner alike!

We wish to make clear that a vote of confidence for officials of the Office of the Prosecutor of the International Criminal Court is in no way a vote of no-confidence in our Philippine investigators and prosecutors. In fact, it is our understanding that because of the principle of complementarity, the International Criminal Court does not exercise its jurisdiction when the organs of a State are willing and able to investigate, to prosecute, to try and to punish, where punishment may be merited.

Our sense of nationhood cannot be so fragile that it cannot allow the entry of persons clothed with international authority to make a determination for themselves that our agencies of law enforcement and prosecution are willing and able to prosecute and to try persons responsible for what can only be characterized as truly heinous assaults on human life.

If we have faith in ourselves and in our institutions, then we should not hesitate about allowing officials of the International Criminal Tribunal to see for themselves that we are able to bring the culpable before the Bar of Justice.

From the Cathedral of St. John the Evangelist, Dagupan City, Pangasinan, October 25, 2023

✠SOCRATES B. VILLEGAS
Archbishop of Lingayen-Dagupan

ARCHBISHOP'S HOUSE
Jovellanos Street, Dagupan City 2400
Pangasinan, Philippines
Telephone: 075 523 5357 • Telefax: 075 522 1878

(enhanced text below)

ARCHDIOCESE OF LINGAYEN-DAGUPAN STATEMENT ON THE ENTRY OF OFFICIALS OF THE INTERNATIONAL CRIMINAL COURT INTO THE PHILIPPINES

The Church always strives after and cherishes the truth. She proclaims her faith, after all, that saving Truth was made Incarnate in the Man from Nazareth, executed because he dared proclaim the truth to those who preferred the shadow of untruth and ignorance.

It is our understanding that the Prosecutor of the International Criminal Court with its seat at The Hague has sought ingress into the country to pursue inquiry and investigation into the deaths and extrajudicial executions that occurred at the height of the past Administration's "war on drugs".

Insofar as this process seeks to ferret out the truth and, possibly, to hold accountable those who, in an arrogant abuse of power, may have caused others, even possibly innocent people, loss of life in violation of guarantees enshrined in the Philippine Constitution as well as in human rights treaties to which the Philippines is a party, a thorough inquiry by persons without vested interests or prior alliances should be welcome. Truth has never destroyed a nation. It is falsehood that has been the undoing of many peoples.

We understand the concerns that have been voiced about what may appear to be a transgression of Philippine sovereignty. However, allowing the investigators and factfinders in can and should be an act of sovereignty a choice we, as a people, freely make for the sake of truth and to vindicate those who may have lost their lives, denied by processes of law that every democracy guarantees both to citizen and foreigner alike!

We wish to make clear that a vote of confidence for officials of the Office of the Prosecutor of the International Criminal Court is in no way a vote of no-confidence in our Philippine investigators and prosecutors. In fact, it is our understanding that because of the principle of complementarity, the International Criminal Court does not exercise its jurisdiction when the organs of a State are willing and able to investigate, to prosecute, to try and to punish, where punishment may be merited.

Our sense of nationhood cannot be so fragile that it cannot allow the entry of persons clothed with international authority to make a determination for themselves that our agencies of law enforcement and prosecution are willing and able to prosecute and to try persons responsible for what can only be characterized as truly heinous assaults on human life. If we have faith in ourselves and in our institutions, then we should not hesitate about allowing officials of the International Criminal Tribunal to see for themselves that we are able to bring the culpable before the Bar of Justice.

From the Cathedral of St. John the Evangelist, Dagupan City, Pangasinan, October 25, 2023

SOCRATES B. VILLEGAS Archbishop of Lingayen-Dagupan
ARCHBISHOP'S HOUSE Jovellanos Street, Dagupan City 2400 Pangasinan, Philippines Telephone: 075 523 5357. Telefax: 075 522 1878

....

2
PAUL HARVEY'S LETTER TO HIS GRANDCHILDREN – posted by Emma Isabella at facebook – Fifty Shades of Life – Oct. 25, 2023

We tried so hard to make things better for our kids that we made them worse. For my grandchildren, I'd like better.

I'd really like for them to know about hand me down clothes and homemade ice cream and leftover meat loaf sandwiches.. I really would.

I hope you learn humility by being humiliated, and that you learn honesty by being cheated.

I hope you learn to make your own bed and mow the lawn and wash the car.

And I really hope nobody gives you a brand new car when you are sixteen.

It will be good if at least one time you can see puppies born and your old dog put to sleep.

I hope you get a black eye fighting for something you believe in.

I hope you have to share a bedroom with your younger brother/sister. And it's all right if you have to draw a line down the middle of the room, but when he wants to crawl under the covers with you because he's scared, I hope you let him.

When you want to see a movie and your little brother/sister wants to tag along, I hope you'll let him/her.

I hope you have to walk uphill to school with your friends and that you live in a town where you can do it safely.

On rainy days when you have to catch a ride, I hope you don't ask your driver to drop you two blocks away so you won't be seen riding with someone as uncool as your Mom.

If you want a slingshot, I hope your Dad teaches you how to make one instead of buying one.

I hope you learn to dig in the dirt and read books.

When you learn to use computers, I hope you also learn to add and subtract in your head.

I hope you get teased by your friends when you have your first crush on a boy/girl, and when you talk back to your mother that you learn what ivory soap tastes like.

May you skin your knee climbing a mountain, burn your hand on a stove, and stick your tongue on a frozen flagpole.

I don't care if you try a beer once, but I hope you don't like it... And if a friend offers you dope or a joint, I hope you realize he/she is not your friend.

I sure hope you make time to sit on a porch with your Grandma/Grandpa and go fishing with your Uncle.

May you feel sorrow at a funeral and joy during the holidays.

I hope your mother punishes you when you throw a baseball through your neighbor's window and that she hugs you and kisses you at Christmas time when you give her a plaster mold of your hand.

These things I wish for you are tough times and disappointment, hard work, and happiness. To me, it's the only way to appreciate life.

....

3
Henry Syr Sr – by Teresita Sy-Coson – Oct. 2023

Sixty-five years ago, my father, Henry Sy, Sr., opened a small shoe store in downtown Manila

It was in October 1958, and at that time he thought, "If I could sell a pair of shoes to every Filipino, I would be a successful man."

But he did so much more than that. With his vision, passion to succeed, and hard work, the company has grown over the years and is now a publicly listed company in retail, property, banking, and portfolio investments.

My siblings and I were growing up when my father started his business. We had front-row seats to his extraordinary way of doing things. He has been our mentor, teaching us about business and life through coaching and through his example. Let me share some of these with you, one value at a time.

My father taught us that it was important to have a great passion to achieve. The adversities of World War II deprived my father of a quality education. However, knowing that education would make him go far, he pursued a college degree but had to stop after two years.

Opportunities were open for him to see the world; hence, he had to make a choice of going back to school or traveling to broaden his knowledge. He chose the latter.

Apart from intelligence and education, it is passion that makes a difference. It increases one's willpower. It is, in fact, the fuel for the will. Passion makes the impossible possible.

Your desires, he believed, determine your destiny. The stronger your willpower to achieve, the greater your potential. If you follow your passion, you become a more dedicated and productive person.

Tatay Jobo Comment: I remember Shoemart Store in Carriedo during the years around 1958. I studied in Mapua Tech during those years and bought my shoes there. I recall a guy who attended to me there, who resembled Henry Sy Sr. The lanky tall Chinese-looking guy actually placed the shoes on my feet and I could not be mistaken.

....

4
The Storyteller – Thanks to those soldiers who served their country – Author Unknown

(Photo with the article by author unknown)

Richard, (my husband), never really talked a lot about his time in Vietnam, other than he had been shot by a sniper. However, he had a rather grainy, 8 x 10 black and white photo he had taken at a USO show of Ann Margret with Bob Hope in the background that was one of his treasures.

A few years ago, Ann Margaret was doing a book signing at a local bookstore. Richard wanted to see if he could get her to Sign the treasured photo so he arrived at the bookstore at 12 o'clock for the 7:30 signing.

When I got there after work, the line went all the way around the bookstore, circled the parking lot, and disappeared behind a parking garage. Before her appearance, bookstore employees announced that she would sign only her book and no memorabilia would be permitted.

Richard was disappointed, but wanted to show her the photo and let her know how much those shows meant to lonely GI's so far from home. Ann Margaret came out looking as beautiful as ever and, as second in line, it was soon Richard's turn.

He presented the book for her signature and then took out the photo. When he did, there were many shouts from the employees that she would not sign it. Richard said,

"I understand. I just wanted her to see it."

She took one look at the photo, tears welled up in her eyes and she said,

"This is one of my gentlemen from Vietnam and I most certainly will sign his photo. I know what these men did for their country and I always have time for 'my gentlemen."

With that, she pulled Richard across the table and planted a big kiss on him. She then made quite a to-do about the bravery of the young men she met over the years, how much she admired them, and how much she appreciated them. There weren't too many dry eyes among those close enough to hear. She then posed for pictures and acted as if he were the only one there.

That night was a turning point for him. He walked a little straighter and, for the first time in years, was proud to have been a Vet. I'll never forget Ann Margaret for her graciousness and how much that small act of kindness meant to my husband.

Later at dinner, Richard was very quiet. When I asked if he'd like to talk about it, my big, strong husband broke down in tears.

"That's the first time anyone ever thanked me for my time in the Army," he said.

I now make it a point to say 'Thank you' to every person I come across who served in our Armed Forces. Freedom does not come cheap and I am grateful for all those who have served their country.

If you'd like to pass on this story, feel free to do so. Perhaps it will help others to become aware of how important it is to acknowledge the contribution our service people make.

~ Original Author Unknown (credits)

....

5
THE LAST LEG OF LIFE!
- Raul Benedicto Manapat
– Nov. 1, 2023

Most of us are now in the last quarter of our life and should read this interesting piece of article.

This is one of the nicest and most gentle articles I've read in a while: No politics, No religion and No racial issues - just food for thought.

You know, time has a way of moving quickly and catching you unaware of the passing years.

It seems just yesterday that I was young and embarking on my new life. Yet, in a way, it seems like years ago, and I wonder where all the years went ?

I know that I lived them all.

I have glimpses of how it was back then and of all my hopes and dreams.

However, here it is, the last quarter of my life and it catches me by surprise !!!

How did I get here so fast ??

Where did the years go and where did my youth go??

I remember well, seeing older people through the years and thinking that those older people were years away from me and that I was only on the first quarter and that the fourth quarter was so far off that I could not visualise it or imagine fully what it would be like.

Yet, here it is !! My friends are retired and getting grey, they move slower and I see an older person now. Some are in better and some worse shape than me, but I see the great change. They're not like the ones that I remember who were young and vibrant. But, like me, their age is beginning to show and we are now those older folks that we used to see and never thought we'd become.

Each day now, I find that just getting a shower is a real target for the day and taking a nap is not a treat anymore !! It's mandatory because if I don't of my own free will, I fall asleep where I sit.

And so, now I enter into this new season of my life unprepared for all the aches and pains and the loss of strength and ability to go and do things that I wish I had done, but never did. At least now I know that, though I'm on the last quarter and I'm not sure how long it will last, that when it's over on this earth, it's all over. A new adventure will begin, I feel !!

Yes, I have regrets. There are things I wish I hadn't done; things I should have done, but truly there are many things I'm happy to have done. It's all in a lifetime.

So, if you're not on the last quarter yet, let me remind you that it will be here faster than you think. So, whatever you would like to accomplish in your life do it quickly.

Don't put things off too long. Life goes by so quickly.

So, do what you can today, as you can never be sure whether you're on the last quarter or not.

You have no promise that you will see all the seasons of life. So, live for today and say all the things that you want your loved ones to remember - and hope that they appreciate and love you for all the things that you have done for them in all the past years.

'Life' is a gift to you. Be Happy !!

Have a great day !!

Remember, it is health that is real wealth and not pieces of gold, silver or printed Notes or even property.

You may think:

Going out is good - but coming back home is much better !!!

You forget names - but it's okay because some people forgot they even knew you !!!

You realize, you are never going to be really good at anything like golf - but you like the outdoors. So, do it.

The things you used to care to do, you aren't as interested in anymore - but, you really don't care that you aren't as interested.

You sleep better on a lounge chair with the TV on than in bed – you call it 'pre-sleep' !!! If you enjoy it, just do it.

You miss the days when everything worked with just an 'On' and 'Off' switch !!!

You tend to use more 4 letter words – 'what' and 'when' ?

You have lots of clothes in your wardrobe, more than half of which you will never wear – but just in case !!

Old is good -
• Old is comfortable.
• Old is safe.
• Old songs.
• Old movies.
• and - best of all,
• Friends of old !!!

So, stay well, 'Old friend.'

Have a fantastic day.

Have an awesome Quarter, whichever one you're in !!!

Take care.

Send this on to other "Old Friends" and let them be smiling in agreement.

It's not what you gather, but what you scatter that tells what kind of life you have lived.
🍷 Cheers 🍷

....

6
FREE LEILA DE LIMA NOW –
posted Nov. 2, 2023

In its Decision adopted unanimously at its 212th Session last 27 Oct. 2023, the Inter-Parliamentary Union (IPU) Governing Council, declares, in part:

"Expresses grave concern that more than seven years after she was first charged, Ms. de Lima continues to languish in detention, even though the prosecution's case has collapsed and the latest recantations of witnesses underscore the serious deficiencies that had already been identified early on in the evidence presented against her."

#FreeLeilaNow

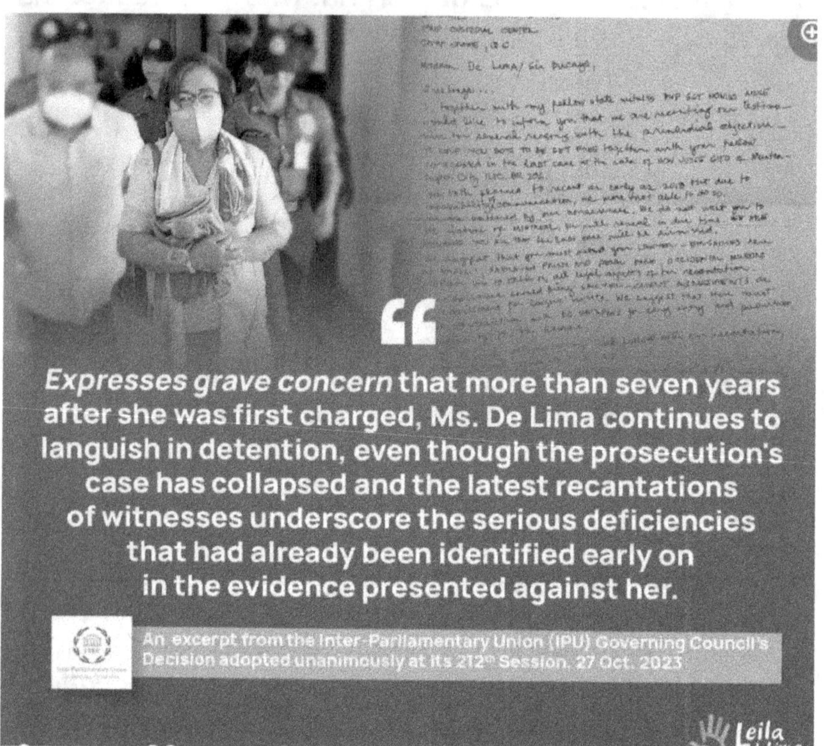
Expresses grave concern that more than seven years after she was first charged, Ms. De Lima continues to languish in detention, even though the prosecution's case has collapsed and the latest recantations of witnesses underscore the serious deficiencies that had already been identified early on in the evidence presented against her.

An excerpt from the Inter-Parliamentary Union (IPU) Governing Council's Decision adopted unanimously at its 212th Session, 27 Oct. 2023

Leila de Lima

Inter-Parliamentary Union
For democracy. For everyone.

Philippines

Decision adopted unanimously by the IPU Governing Council at its 212th session (Luanda, 27 October 2023)

Former Philippine senator and human rights campaigner Leila de Lima (centre) waves as she arrives at the Muntinlupa City Trial Court in Manila on 16 October 2023. | JAM STA ROSA / AFP

PHL-08 – Leila de Lima

Alleged human rights violations

- Threats, acts of intimidation
- Arbitrary arrest and detention
- Lack of due process in proceedings against parliamentarians
- Violation of freedom of opinion and expression

A. Summary of the case

Ms. Leila de Lima served as Chairperson of the Philippines Commission on Human Rights from May 2008 to June 2010. In that capacity, she led a series of investigations into alleged extrajudicial killings linked to the so-called Davao Death Squad in Davao City, where Mr. Duterte had been long-time mayor, and concluded that Mr. Duterte, former President of the Philippines, was behind the Davao Death Squad.

In 2010, Ms. de Lima was appointed Secretary of Justice. She resigned from this position in October 2015 to focus on her campaign for a senate seat in the May 2016 elections, a bid that was successful. In August 2016, as Chair of the Senate Committee on Justice and Human Rights, she launched an inquiry into the killings of thousands of alleged drug users and drug dealers, which had reportedly taken place after President Duterte took office in June 2016. After she was elected to the Senate, she

Case PHL-08

Philippines: Parliament affiliated to the IPU

Victim: Female opposition member of parliament

Qualified complainant(s): Section I(1)(a) of the Committee Procedure (Annex I)

Submission of complaint: September 2016

Recent IPU decision: February 2023

Recent IPU mission: May 2017

Recent Committee hearing(s): -----

Recent follow-up:
- Communication from the authorities: Letter from the Director General of the Office of International Relations and Protocol of the Senate and Secretary of the IPU Group of the Philippines (April 2021)
- Communication from the complainant: October 2023
- Communication to the authorities: Letter to the President of the Senate (September 2023)
- Communication to the complainant: October 2023

became the target of acts of intimidation and denigration, including by the then President Duterte himself.

On 7 November 2016, Ms. de Lima filed a petition for writ of *habeas data* against the then President Duterte before the Supreme Court, requesting that the Court, *inter alia*, order President Duterte and any of his representatives to cease: seeking details about her private life outside the realm of legitimate public concern or making statements maligning her as a woman and injuring her dignity as a human being; discriminating against her on the basis of gender; describing or publicizing her alleged sexual conduct; engaging in psychological violence against her; and otherwise violating her rights or engaging in acts that are contrary to law, good morals, good customs, public policy and/or public interest. On 18 October 2019, the Supreme Court dismissed the petition for writ of *habeas data* on the grounds that the President is immune from suit during his incumbency and tenure.

Ms. de Lima was arrested and detained on 24 February 2017 over accusations of receiving drug money to finance her campaign for a senate seat. The charges, in three different cases, were brought in the wake of an inquiry by the House of Representatives into drug trading in New Bilibid Prison, and Ms. de Lima's responsibility in such trading while she was Secretary of Justice. The House-led inquiry was launched one week after she initiated her inquiry in the Senate into the extrajudicial killings.

Since July 2018, Ms. de Lima has been charged in the three cases before Branches 205 and 256 of the Regional Trial Court (RTC) – Muntinlupa City. On 17 February 2021, RTC Branch 205 granted Ms. de Lima's demurrer to evidence in case No. 17-166, technically acquitting her, in the absence of sufficient evidence.

The complainant points out that during the presentation of the prosecution's evidence in the first of the two remaining cases (Case No. 17-165), not only was there no physical evidence of the alleged illegal drugs, or the money allegedly delivered to Ms. de Lima as her share in the alleged illegal drug trade, but even the prosecution's own witnesses, mostly criminals serving sentences in the New Bilibid Prison, denied any involvement or even any personal knowledge of the alleged illegal drug trade. Instead, the prosecution spent most of its time attempting to prove the guilt of its own witnesses, including Mr. Peter Co, Mr. Hans Tan and Mr. Vicente Sy, all of whom repeatedly denied any involvement in the illegal drug trade, and whom the prosecution, to this date, has failed to indict as co-conspirators. Conveniently, the only person who was consistently singled out by these witnesses as having personal knowledge of the New Bilibid Prison drug trade and the role of Ms. de Lima died on 26 September 2016. That person, Mr. Tony Co, was an inmate who was stabbed to death in a staged prison riot that targeted inmates who initially refused to testify against Ms. de Lima before the House of Representatives Justice Committee's hearing on the New Bilibid Prison drug trade. Most importantly, the complainant points out that the prosecution's foremost witness in the case, Mr. Rafael Ragos, former National Bureau of Investigation Deputy Director and former Bureau of Corrections Officer-in-Charge, who had been the sole witness to testify that he had delivered money to Ms. de Lima's house on two occasions, recanted all his testimonies and statements against Ms. de Lima on 30 April 2022. In his retraction, Mr. Ragos said that he had been forced to testify against her by the then Secretary of Justice Vitaliano Aguirre II, who had led the witch hunt against Ms. de Lima in the Philippines' House of Representatives Justice Committee's hearings in 2016. In light of Mr. Ragos' recantation of his testimony, Case No. 17-165 was concluded on 12 May 2023 with the acquittal of Ms. de Lima, but the Office of the Solicitor General and the Department of Justice appealed the acquittal to the Court of Appeals, according to the complainant, in violation of the constitutional proscription against double jeopardy.

After Mr. Ragos' recantation, and earlier recantations by Mr. Kerwin Espinosa and co-accused former bodyguard Mr. Ronnie Dayan, in the remaining case (Case No. 17-167), two more witnesses for the prosecution recanted their testimony on 16 October 2023. This was done in a letter handed over to Ms. de Lima, and subsequently shared with the court, in which they said that they were "bothered by their consciences" and that they did not want the accused to be a victim of mistrial. The letter also mentioned that five more witnesses would also recant. Moreover, the complainant underscores that at least two other witnesses, Mr. Joel Capones and Mr. Herbert Colanggo, claim to have engaged in illegal drug trading. Despite these admissions made under oath and in open court, to this day the prosecution has actively refused to charge them, whether as co-conspirators in the same case or in a separate case, hence showing – according to the complainant – that they stand to benefit from incriminating Ms. de Lima. Currently, the case is pending before the RTC of Muntinlupa City (Branch 206), with Judge Gener Gito presiding. Pending before the court is the motion for reconsideration of the court order under the previous judge, Mr. Romeo Buenaventura, who denied Ms. de Lima's

- 3 -

application for bail on 7 June 2023. The motion for reconsideration was put forward after it was discovered that Judge Buenaventura's brother had direct and close links to the president of the aforementioned House of Representatives inquiry into Ms. de Lima in 2016. The complainant states that the court case is moving at a snail's pace and that only one day of every following month, at least until March 2024, will be dedicated to further hearings. A motion for reconsideration of the defence counsel's petition for bail is pending before the current judge. At the hearing on 16 October 2023, the prosecution concluded the presentation of its evidence-in-chief. The court gave the prosecution 20 days to file their formal offer of evidence. The same number of days was given to the defence counsel to file any comments/opposition thereto.

On 30 November 2018, the United Nations Working Group on Arbitrary Detention concluded, echoing the conclusions of an earlier IPU mission to the Philippines, that Senator de Lima's detention was arbitrary and that her immediate release was in order.

Ms. de Lima ran for re-election to the Senate from detention in the elections held in May 2022, but was not re-elected.

B.   Decision

The Committee on the Human Rights of Parliamentarians

1.   *Expresses* grave *concern* that more than seven years after she was first charged, Ms. de Lima continues to languish in detention, even though the prosecution's case has collapsed and the latest recantations of witnesses underscore the serious deficiencies that had already been identified early on in the evidence presented against her;

2.   *Remains convinced* that the steps taken against Ms. De Lima came in response to her vocal opposition to the way in which the then President Duterte was waging war on drugs, including her denunciation of his alleged responsibility for extrajudicial killings; and *points out* in this regard the inexplicable length of the criminal proceedings, the repeated violation of the principle of the presumption of innocence, the timing of the criminal proceedings, the amendment of the charges, the reliance on testimonies of convicted drug traffickers, who were either given favourable treatment in return, subjected to physical intimidation, including death, in prison, or have an axe to grind against Ms. De Lima as a result of her efforts to dismantle their drug trafficking operations when she was Secretary of Justice, and the pressure exerted on other individuals to testify against her;

3.   *Renews it call,* in light of the foregoing, for Ms. de Lima to be released immediately and for the remaining criminal case against her to be dropped; and *urges* the authorities to take the necessary action forthwith;

4.   *Requests* the Secretary General to convey this decision to the President of the Philippines, the relevant parliamentary authorities, the complainant and any third party likely to be in a position to supply relevant information;

5.   *Requests* the Committee to continue examining this case and to report back to it in due course.

....

7

Scientific Death of Jesus – by The Revival – Nov. 8, 2023 – posted at facebook

For the next 60 seconds, set aside whatever you're doing and take this opportunity! Let's see if Satan can stop this.

At the age of 33, Jesus was condemned to death.

At the time, crucifixion was the "worst" death. Only the worst criminals were condemned to be crucified. Yet it was even more dreadful for Jesus. Unlike other criminals condemned to death by crucifixion, Jesus was to be nailed to the cross by His hands and feet.

Each nail was 6 to 8 inches long.

The nails were driven into His wrist, not into His palms as is commonly portrayed. There's a tendon in the wrist that extends to the shoulder. The Roman guards knew that when the nails were being hammered into the wrist, that tendon would tear and break, forcing Jesus to use His back muscles to support Himself so that He could breathe.

Both of His feet were nailed together. Thus He was forced to support Himself on the single nail that impaled His feet to the cross. Jesus could not support Himself with His legs because of the pain so He was forced to alternate between arching His back then using His legs just to continue to breathe. Imagine the struggle, the pain, the suffering, the courage.

Jesus endured this reality for over 3 hours.

Yes, over 3 hours! Can you imagine this kind of suffering? A few minutes before He died,

Jesus stopped bleeding. He was simply pouring water from his wounds.

From common images we see wounds to His hands and feet and even the spear wound to His side... But do we realize His wounds were actually made in his body. A hammer driving large nails through the wrist, the feet overlapped and an even larger nail hammered through the arches, then a Roman guard piercing His side with a spear. But before the nails and the spear, Jesus was whipped and beaten. The whipping was so severe that it tore the flesh from His body. The beating so horrific that His face was torn and his beard ripped from His face. The crown of thorns cut deeply into His scalp. Most men would not have survived this torture.

He had no more blood to bleed out, only water poured from His wounds. The human adult body contains about 3.5 liters (just less than a gallon) of blood.

Jesus poured all 3.5 liters of his blood; He had three nails hammered into His members; a crown of thorns on His head and, beyond that, a Roman soldier who stabbed a spear into His chest..

All these without mentioning the humiliation He suffered after carrying His own cross for almost 2 kilometers, while the crowd spat in his face and threw stones (the cross was almost 30 kg of weight, only for its higher part, where His hands were nailed).

Jesus had to endure this experience, to open the gates of Heaven, so that you can have free access to God.

So that your sins could be "washed" away. All of them, with no exception! Don't ignore this situation.

JESUS CHRIST DIED FOR YOU!

He died for you! It is easy to pass jokes or foolish photos by e-mail, but when it comes to God, sometimes you feel ashamed to forward to others because you are worried of what they may think about you.

God has plans for you, show all your friends what He experienced to save you. Now think about this! May God bless your life!

If you are not ashamed to do this, please, follow Jesus' instructions. He said (Matthew 10:32 & 33): "Everyone therefore who acknowledges me before others, I also will acknowledge

before My Father in heaven; but whosoever denies Me before others, I will deny before My Father in heaven.

8

Subject: 1st Email: BANGKO SENTRAL MUST FIGHT INFLATION IN VENUES OUTSIDE THE BANKING SYSTEM - MARCELO L. TECSON - A CPA and Concerned Citizen - Good Governance Advocate – Nov.14, 2023

----- Forwarded Message -----

From: Marcelo Tecson <martecson@yahoo.com>

To: President Ferdinand Marcos Jr <pace@malacanang.gov.ph>; BSP Governor Eli Remolona <bspmail@bsp.gov.ph>; DOF Sec Benjamin Diokno <secfin@dof.gov.ph>

Cc: Senate Pres. Juan Miguel Zubiri <senmigzzubiri@gmail.com>; Speaker Ferdinand Martin Romualdez <speaker@martinromualdez.ph>; Socioeconomic Planning Sec Arsenio Balisacan <osec@neda.gov.ph>; DOE Sec Raphael Lotilla <rlotilla@doe.gov.ph>; DTI Sec Alfredo Pascual <secretary@dti.gov.ph>; Office of the DOF Chief Economist <oce@dof.gov.ph>; Senator Loren Legarda <loren@lorenlegarda.com.ph>; Senator Joel Villanueva <senatorjoelvillanueva@yahoo.com>; Senator Koko Pimentel <senatorkoko@kokopimentel.org>; Senator Sonny Angara <sensonnyangara@yahoo.com>; Senator Nancy Binay <binaynancy2013@yahoo.com>; Senator Raffy Tulfo <raffy.tulfo@teamtulfo.com>; Senator Alan Peter Cayetano <alanpeter@cayetano.com.ph>; Senator Pia Cayetano <pia@piacayetano.ph>; Senator Ronald dela Rosa <secretariat.batodelarosa@gmail.com>; Senator Joseph

Victor Ejercito <publicassistance@jvejercito.com>; Senator Francis Escudero <senator@chizescudero.com>; Senator Jinggoy Ejercito Estrada <senatorjinggoyestrada@gmail.com>; Senator Win Gatchalian <email@wingatchalian.com>; Senator Bong Go <media@senatorbonggo.ph>; Senator Risa Hontiveros <risahq@gmail.com>; Senator Manuel Lapid <manuellitolapid@gmail.com>; Senator Grace Poe <gracepoe2013@gmail.com>; Senator Francis Tolentino <tolsenate@gmail.com>; Senator Cynthia Villar <sencynthiavillar@gmail.com>; Senator Mark Villar <markvillarofficial@gmail.com>; Senator Robin Padilla <osrobinpadilla@gmail.com>; Senator Imee Marcos <osimeemarcos@gmail.com>; Senator Ramon Bong Revilla Jr. <senbongrevilla2019@gmail.com>; Senate Economic Planning Office <sepo@senate.gov.ph>; Rep. Joey Salceda <joey.salceda@house.gov.ph>; Rep. France Castro <france.castro@house.gov.ph>; Congressional Policy and Budget Office <cpbo_hor@yahoo.com>; Philippine Institute of CPAs <admin_dept@picpa.com.ph>; CHED Chairperson <chairperson@ched.gov.ph>; Philippine Economic Society <pes.eaea@gmail.com>; Foundation for Economic Freedom <fef@fef.org.ph>; IBON Media & Communications <ibonfoundation@gmail.com>; Philippine Institute for Development Studies <pids-op@pids.gov.ph>; Oxfam Philippines <infoph@oxfam.org.uk>; VERA Files <newsroom@verafiles.org>; The Rappler Team <info@rappler.com>; SUKI <suki-network@googlegroups.com>; Cenpeg <cenpeg.info@gmail.com>; Peter Angelo Perfecto <pvperfecto@gmail.com>; Office of the Dean <ncpag_dean.upd@up.edu.ph>; UP NCPAG Dean <dean_up_ncpag@yahoo.com>; Dan Saguil <dasaguil@yahoo.com>; Solita Monsod <solita_monsod@yahoo.com>; Cielito Habito <cielito.habito@gmail.com>; Felipe Medalla <plcmedalla@yahoo.com>; Calixto Chikiamko <fefphilippines@gmail.com>; Ronald Mendoza

<ronmendoza@gmail.com>; Raul Fabella <raul.fabella@up.edu.ph>; Bernardo Villegas <bernardo.villegas@uap.asia>; Gerardo Sicat <gpsicat@gmail.com>; V. Abola <vabola@gmail.com>; Peter U <peteru@uap.asia>; Alvin Ang <angalvinp@gmail.com>; E. De Dios <esdedios@up.edu.ph>; Rolando Dy <rdyster@gmail.com>; Teresa Tadem <teresatadem@gmail.com>; Fe Mangahas <fbmangahas@hotmail.com>; "dante.canlas@up.edu.ph" <dante.canlas@up.edu.ph>; "romeo.lopez.bernardo@gmail.com" <romeo.lopez.bernardo@gmail.com>; varsitar@yahoo.com <varsitar@yahoo.com>; michael.alba@gmail.com <michael.alba@gmail.com>; naldaba@gmail.com <naldaba@gmail.com>; filomenoiii@yahoo.com <filomenoiii@yahoo.com>; Sonny Sioson <stsioson@gmail.com>; Jr. Rodolfo Javellana <saveearth_20@yahoo.com>; Butch Junia <philconsumerforum@gmail.com>

Sent: Tuesday, November 14, 2023 at 05:38:06 PM GMT+8

Subject: 1st Email: BANGKO SENTRAL MUST FIGHT INFLATION IN VENUES OUTSIDE THE BANKING SYSTEM

**BANGKO SENTRAL MUST
THINK OUTSIDE THE BOX AND
FIGHT INFLATION IN VENUES
OUTSIDE THE BANKING SYSTEM**

**INTRODUCTION:
BSP HAS FAILED TO WAGE
HALF OF THE ANTI-INFLATION WAR**

BSP'S Mandate: Price Stability

Under Chapter 1, Section 3 of The New Central Bank Act (RA 7653, approved on June 14, 1993), the primary objective of Bangko Sentral ng Pilipinas (Bangko Sentral or BSP) is to maintain PRICE STABILITY. Thus, the BSP Governor and Department of Finance (DOF) Secretary, together with their co-members in the BSP Monetary Board, are mandated to stabilize prices and tame INFLATION.

Under Section 5 on Corporate Powers of the same law, BSP officials are authorized to perform any and all things (or acts) necessary or proper to carry out the purposes of RA 7653. Unfortunately, they and their predecessors have FAILED TO THINK OUTSIDE THE BOX and apparently confined their work to only those taught in BUSINESS SCHOOLS, such as applying tight-money policy tools in the banking system to reduce money supply and rein in inflation. Their failure has caused unlawful approval of WRONG rate INCREASES or INFLATION in VENUES outside the banking system: Energy Regulatory Commission (ERC), MWSS, Toll Regulatory Board (TRB), Wholesale Electricity Spot Market (WESM), and National Telecommunication Commission (NTC).

BSP Grievously Erred
In the 1997-1998 Asian Crisis at the
Price of 36% Bad Loans to Borrowers:
 It Fought Dollar Speculation through
Bad-Loan Provoking 32% High Interest Rate,
Instead of Enforcing its Available Bad-Loan-Free

1962 Anti-Speculation REGULATION, Simply
Because BSP Officials Failed to Fathom and
Recognize that their REGULATION (EXHIBIT 9)-

First Suggested to BSP Under my April 1, 1998

Letter Personally Transmitted to it (EXHIBIT 7)-

Was Already the Missing SOLUTION to Currency
Speculation, Which 17 Central Bank Chiefs from
Around the Globe Who Met in Hong Kong in January 1999 Failed to Find (EXHIBIT 6)

BSP officials must be open-minded on constructive suggestions from the public because BSP does not necessarily perform quite well in its primary job of maintaining PRICE STABILITY or taming INFLATION. Contrary to common notion, it did not perform well in the 1997-1998 Asian crisis. *It was terribly wrong in raising its key policy rate to 32% right on the onset of crisis on July 11, 1997, thereby giving the cue to local banks to promptly raise their interest rate to the same 32% or even higher, eventually peaking at roughly 40%, with consequent staggering* ▯600-billion *or 36% BAD LOANS in the Philippine banking system, initially estimated at 32% by the international consultancy firm, Ernst & Young (EXHIBIT 3).*

BSP's more than 30% disastrous but inefficacious very high interest rate was intended to "ward off (dollar) speculators." (EXHIBIT 1). However, such ultra high lending rate was unnecessary because, as it eventually turned out after my repeated recommendation to BSP officials—which started with my April 1, 1998 letter to BSP (EXHIBIT 7)—I accidentally learned that *BSP has an still effective antique but updated 1962 REGULATION or circular against currency speculation (EXHIBIT 9). It was inherited from the defunct Central Bank of the Philippines, but unrecognized as anti-speculation regulation and unimplemented by our new crop of central bankers even when needed most during the 1997-1998 Asian meltdown.*

After my reminding BSP about its overlooked 1962 REGULATION and doing repeated follow-ups—such as that shown in the 4th email—when BSP was constrained to heed my recommendation by enforcing its old and updated REGULATION through running after and penalizing erring banks (EXHIBITS 9-11), the peso suddenly appreciated from ☐53.05 to ☐51.85 to the US dollar (EXHIBIT 12). These events are treated at length in my coming 3rd and 4th emails.

**BSP Has Continued to Err
In Using High Interest Rate
in the Performance of its Primary
Mandate to Contain Inflation**

This is the first of four emails on why Bangko Sentral's present use of high interest rate in taming inflation seems WRONG, and why its being WRONG is probable because it had been terribly WRONG on the same high-interest-rate solution against currency speculation and inflation during the 1997-1998 Asian crisis. However, as the probability of BSP's being WRONG is hard to believe, the emails are detailed and long to anticipate the expected disagreement and counterarguments by BSP's officials and technical experts on my unflattering conclusions.

In brief, BSP's present high-interest-rate solution vs. inflation is WRONG because it is a bomb-approach that kills both military targets and innocent civilians, instead of sniper-approach that kills only the targeted enemy officials, without collateral damage to civilians.

For example, this 1st email shows that BSP's high-interest-rate solution is applied—*at the price of harmful high interest rate to beneficial investor-borrowers*—even against INFLATION that does not necessarily harm the generally poor mass consumers because the products with INFLATION are not basic needs. These are dispensable and consumers can shift to cheap substitutes or forego purchase altogether, such as that on deregulated non-essential and luxury products with elastic demand (price increase reduces demand and vice versa).

On the other hand, the INFLATION that harms mass consumers, yet cannot be countered or affected by BSP's high-interest-rate cure because prices are REGULATED, that on basic necessities—like power, water, and tollway services with inelastic demand (price increase does not reduce demand because consumers cannot do without the basic-necessity products)—is totally overlooked and not addressed by BSP.

Because BSP does not do anything against INFLATION arising from VENUES outside the banking system, that from WRONGLY approved OVERPRICING by government regulatory offices—particularly ERC, MWSS, and TRB—it may not be aware of the technically WRONG justification for power, water, and tollway rate increases under the performance-based-regulation (PBR) rate-setting method, which is in violation of the RULE under laws (like Section 12 of the MWSS Charter, RA 6234) that provide for rate of return based on ASSETS already existing and in use or in OPERATION. The RULE clearly disallows as basis of price hike the ground for rate increase under PBR—still unspent FUTURE CAPITAL EXPENDITURES.

As explained in Chapter 14 of my book, *Inequality: Economic Tyranny* (2022 edition), overpricing from double billing arises when, upon completion of each capital project financed by consumers through rate increase under PBR, the cost of the completed project (recorded as owned by the public service company because the rate increase for the project is recorded as regular sales or income, not trust account earmarked for the project) is recovered again from consumers as DEPRECIATION expense, with 12% allowable return to boot—even if the completed project was already paid for by consumers through a prior rate increase.

Other major CAUSES of OVERPRICING, or unwarranted INFLATION, that BSP should have tried to correct or remedy—but did not—are the following:

1. The use of technically WRONG measure—return on rate base (RORB), with rate base misinterpreted as assets in operation—in reckoning the allowable 12% reasonable return limit of public utilities and other monopoly public service providers. As presented in Chapter 9 of my cited book and select book Highlights, copies of which were personally delivered by my staff to the office of each member of the BSP Monetary Board, the correct measure is return on equity (ROE).

2. Based on a Facebook post by my co-advocate for good governance, Romeo "Butch" Junia, as well as my own observations during ERC hearings, multi-billion-peso understatement in power-rate refunds is quite probable, such as on delayed Meralco 5-year rate rebasing. The shortchanging of consumers on understated refunds constitutes undue INFLATION, or improper OVERPRICING or price increase, that should have been prevented—but was not—by BSP officials mandated to fight INFLATION.

Based on the foregoing major causes of basic-necessity OVERPRICING or undue INFLATION, it appears that the highly regarded Bangko Sentral has not even waged half of the ANTI-INFLATION war—that in VENUES outside the banking system: government regulatory offices improperly approving unjustified rate increases, which yield to public service companies rates of return in breach of the Supreme Court-ruled 12% reasonable return limit.

It is Time for BSP to Prevent Basic-Necessity Overpricing or Undue INFLATION in ERC and other Government Regulatory Offices Susceptible to Regulatory Capture

As a retired senior citizen, I intend to stop attending price-increase-petition and related hearings in government regulatory offices, like ERC and MWSS. *It is not right to tolerate failure by anti-inflation BSP people to attend those hearings by having concerned citizens, or civil society groups, do the attending of hearings for them.* It is not right for private citizens to do the BSP officials' job that they do not do. The BSP officials must do it now. Otherwise, let them be accountable to Malacañang, Congress, and the people for their failure to really do what it takes to neutralize INFLATION.

In doing their job, BSP officials must focus on INFLATION of basic necessities in VENUEs outside the banking system because, firstly, it is included in—or not exempted from—BSP's price-stability mission. Secondly, it is the kind of inflation that harms most the generally poor mass consumers.

BSP's action is needed to counter the long existing OVERPRICING in approved rates of basic-necessity public utilities and other public services—as concretely evidenced by the public service companies' return on equity (ROE) in breach of the Supreme Court-ruled 12% reasonable return limit for public utilities (ERB vs. Meralco, G.R. No. 141314 dated November 15, 2002, affirmed on April 9, 2003), which must also apply to similarly situated other monopoly public service providers.

Following are examples of public service monopolies with ROE (after tax) in violation of the Supreme Court ruling:

Meralco	Maynilad	NLEX Corp.
(Power)	(Water)	(Tollway)
2016: 26%	2008: 247%	2016: 46%
2017: 28%	2009: 147%	2017: 46%
2018: 28%	2010: 82%	2018: 39%

There is simply no valid legal justification for the foregoing blatant breach of the Supreme Court-ruled 12% profit-rate limit, and yet no government official has so far acted on it.

At their own time, expense, and effort, civil society groups and concerned citizens who are NOT paid and mandated to do so, oppose—usually to no avail for lack of enough resources and competent lawyers—the petitions for unwarranted price increases before regulatory offices seemingly susceptible to regulatory capture.

Therefore, *the BSP Governor and Monetary Board, with mandated price-stability mission, must do the same. They must similarly oppose unjustified public-service rate increases or INFLATION, because they are the ones mandated and highly paid to maintain price stability or fight INFLATION.* They have at their power and command the similarly highly paid economic, finance, and legal experts of the cash-rich and mighty Bangko Sentral. All they have to do is instruct their subordinate officials and experts to do it at government time and expense, yet they have heretofore not done it. *UUtusan lang nila ang mga tauhan nila, hindi pa nila nagawa!*

Thus, it is evident that BSP officials FAILED TO THINK OUTSIDE THE BOX, or innovate, when they confined their anti-inflation work solely in the banking system. They should have helped prevent higher prices emanating from other VENUES of INFLATION: in government regulatory offices, like the Energy Regulatory Commission (ERC), MWSS, the National Telecommunication Commission (NTC), the Toll Regulatory Board (TRB), and the Wholesale Electricity Spot Market (WESM).

**If IN THE PAST, BSP WAS WRONG
ON HIGH INTEREST RATE AGAINST
CURRENCY SPECULATION; TODAY, BASED
ON ITS TRACK RECORD OF FALLIBILITY
ON SOMETHING SO BASIC OR OBVIOUS,
IT IS NOT UNTHINKABLE THAT IT IS ALSO
WRONG ON HIGH INTEREST RATE
AGAINST STUBBORN INFLATION**

High Interest Rate as Monetary Tool
Against Inflation is Fine in Theory, But its
Use Must be Condition-Oriented—Because
It Applies to Some But Not to All Situations

The conventional high-interest-rate economic wisdom is normally employed by monetary authorities to attain the chain objectives of *minimized borrowing, tightened money supply,* discouraged currency speculation, stabilized exchange rate, curbed currency depreciation, and ultimately *contained inflation* (Marcelo L. Tecson, *Puzzlers: Economic Sting* (Makati City, Philippines: Raiders of the Lost Gold Publication, 2005), p. 104).

The high-interest-rate monetary tool, however, must be used sparingly because it has negative side effects. It is counterproductive because it dampens demand and stifles production loans that are essential to economic growth. It also means higher cost of doing business that translates to increase in price or inflation.

As stated at the outset, in the Asian meltdown, BSP grossly misapplied the high-interest-rate tight-money policy tool against currency speculation. Today, as expounded on in this paper, BSP's use of high interest rate—like its latest rate increase—also appears highly misapplied because, first, it is TECHNICALLY WRONG, and, second, there are available BETTER ALTERNATIVES.

UNIMAGINATIVE BSP
HAS CONTINUED TO EMPLOY
HIGH INTEREST RATE AGAINST
INFLATION—INSTEAD OF CONSULTING
SYSTEMS EXPERTS ON THE SEARCH
FOR LESS HARMFUL ALTERNATIVES

Presented here for review purposes are excerpts from two news reports on the reasons for BSP's latest raising further of the already high interest rate.

BSP delivers 'urgent'
anti-inflation rate hike

By Ian Nicolas P. Cigaral
Philippine Daily Inquirer
October 27, 2023, page B1

As its chief had hinted, the Bangko Sentral ng Pilipinas (BSP) resumed hiking its policy rate in an off-cycle decision on Thursday, with the possibility of further tightening in a bid to bring inflation back to target as price pressures continue to build. The Monetary Board (MB) lifted the key rate by 25 basis points to 6.5 percent after what analysts called a "hawkish pause" for four straight meetings.

Banks use the BSP's benchmark rate as guidance when charging interest rates on loans. *By making borrowing costs more expensive, the BSP wants to temper strong demand for commodities with limited supply. This, in effect, tames inflation.*

But there are strong voices like Socioeconomic Planning Secretary Arsenio Balisacan who have pointed out that further rate hikes won't work now because *much of the price pressures are coming from supply problems....*

Rising borrowing costs also mean more expensive debts for the Marcos administration, which has to bridge a projected budget gap of ☐1.5-trillion this year.

PH inflation rose to 6.1%
in September as food prices,
transport cost soared

By Ian Nicolas P. Cigaral
Philippine Daily Inquirer Online
October 5, 2023

Consumer prices rose at a faster rate (to 6.1 percent) in September on the back of higher food prices, likely keeping the pressure on the Bangko Sentral ng Pilipinas to stay hawkish.... The PSA (Philippine Statistics Authority) attributed the increase to higher year-on-year rise in food and non-alcoholic beverages prices at 9.7 percent, up from 8.1 percent in August. Transport (cost) with inflation rate of 1.2 percent during the month, also contributed to the uptrend, it added."

    ----End of Excerpts------

Based on the foregoing backgrounder, BSP's further use of high interest rate in fighting inflation is technically WRONG, as treated in this paper.

WHY BANGKO SENTRAL IS MONUMENTALLY WRONG IN USING HIGH INTEREST RATE AGAINST PERSISTING INFLATION

Arresting rising inflation is a form of problem-solving, under which there are some pointers or guides to follow. In problem-solving, we must find solutions not only to the problem but also to its root or cause, because the problem may be a mere symptom of its cause. If the cause is not addressed, the problem may recur.

In finding solutions, any particular way of solving a problem is just one of many possible ways of doing it. We must explore other ways by restructuring and rearranging the available information to generate alternative patterns, instead of moving in a clearly defined direction towards the perceived solution—as wrongly done in the heretofore resort to conventional high interest rate in fighting inflation, without consulting systems experts on possible less punishing alternative systems or solutions. By looking at the issue in a different light, we may find what we are looking for. This process involves the discipline systems and procedures, not necessarily economics.

In systems work, we challenge and rationalize every important process, every major activity. We ask why something is, or is not, done. We question age-old methods. We look at things in many possible ways, analyze data and information, and generate alternatives—until we find *the elusive one best way of doing things*. The best solution must be EFFECTIVE or attains objective, as well as EFFICIENT or at cheapest cost and with least negative side effects. [Marcelo L. Tecson, *Inequality: Economic Tyranny*, (Quezon City: Central Book Supply, August 2022), p. 437]

Based on the foregoing litmus test of validity and propriety, BSP's further hike in interest rate is TECHNICALLY WRONG because it does not past the test of EFFECTIVENSS and EFFICIENCY, let alone that of being the elusive one best solution to the present high inflation.

GENERAL GUIDES ON
HOW TO FIGHT INFLATION
BASED ON THE UNAPPRECIATED
SYSTEMS-AND-PROCEDURES DISCIPLINE

1. Determine the kind of INFLATION that Bangko Sentral must focus on by segmentizing the goods and services based on their functions into:

a. Products that satisfy human WANTS or caprices and with elastic or flexible demand affected by increase or decrease in prices, under which demand decreases as price increases, and vice versa. As these products are not basic needs, in case of significant price increases, consumers can resort to suitable cheap substitutes or dispense with them altogether. Consequently, Bangko Sentral need fight INFLATION on these products through burdensome high interest rate to borrowers.

b. Products that satisfy human NEEDS and with inelastic or stable demand NOT affected by increase or decrease in prices. As these products are basic necessities which consumers cannot do without, like food and water, these have to be purchased even if there is a price increase.

As the goods and services that satisfy human NEEDS have to be bought and consumed by consumers regardless of price, they cannot avoid the INFLATION on these products. *Therefore, as a general rule, Bangko Sentral must fight the INFLATION on products that satisfy human NEEDS because this is the kind of INFLATION that is unavoidable and harmful to generally poor Filipino mass consumers.*

2. Determine the CAUSES of INFLATION on the products that satisfy human NEEDS. Tracing the ROOT of a problem before directly thinking of SOLUTIONS to it is imperative because the problem may be just a symptom of its root or cause. If the CAUSE is not addressed, the problem will persist.

The root or CAUSE of a problem is the DETERMINANT of the needed SOLUTION, which is NOT necessarily HIGH INTEREST RATE in the case of the inflation problem. The SOLUTION must be determined based on a proper cause-and-effect analysis.

SPECIFIC GUIDES
IN FIGHTING INFLATION

BSP Need Not Fight
Through High Interest Rate—
at the Expense of Productive Industries
and Economic Growth—the INFLATION on
Non-essential and LUXURY Products that
Merely Satisfy Human WANTS and Caprices;
Bigger Tax Collection from High Prices of
Luxury Items is Beneficial to the Economy

BSP need not bother itself on inflation on non-essential and luxury goods and services that satisfy the wants and caprices of the minority rich, as well as others with surplus earnings or disposable income. These are products with elastic demand and the middle class and majority poor can either harmlessly shift to suitable cheap substitutes or forego purchase altogether. Moreover, increased tax collection from inflation on luxury products is even beneficial to the economy.

To illustrate, a company may price a weekend stay in its super-luxury resort at □5 million, or a famous couturier may design an exquisitely beautiful wedding gown at □50 million. Paradoxically, the government need *not* mind the INFLATION from such an ultra-high pricing system because nobody is shortchanged and hurt by it. The rich customers can very well afford the high prices and willingly paid them. Their patronage of the high-price niche market will help perk up the economy as well as increase government tax collection. In other words, through these high-priced transactions, surplus funds from the rich will beneficially flow into businesses, roughly one-third of which will go to the government as 12% VAT and either 20% or 25% corporate income tax, usable in government social spending for the poor and vital public services.

WHAT TO FOCUS ON:
BSP Must Focus on Fighting INFLATION
on BASIC NECESSITIES that Satisfy Human
NEEDS—Because this is What Makes the
Lives of Majority Poor Filipinos Miserable

HOW TO DO IT:
Reining in the Inflation
on a Few Basic Necessities
(About 10 kinds) Must be Done on a
Case-to-Case or Surgical Precision Basis,

Not through BSP's Shotgun Approach
In the Form of High Interest Rate
That Does Not Address the Causes
of Present Inflation

The inflation that hurts mass consumers is that on basic necessities affected with public interest, like food, power, water, public transport, medicines, healthcare, petroleum products, education, tollways, and telecom services.

Raising interest rate intended to dampen inflationary increase in demand on basic necessities will not affect, let alone reduce, their prices— because their high prices are driven by stable DEMAND based on NEED, not by surplus or easy money from low interest rate. *Basic-necessity suppliers' borrowing from banks cannot be discouraged either by BSP-induced increase in interest rate because, in order to maintain their 12% entitlement to a reasonable return on investment, they can readily pass on the interest-rate hike to their consumers.*

For example, in the case of power, water, and tollway services, their rates are regulated with allowable 12% rate of return based on practice and a Supreme Court ruling (ERB vs. Meralco. G.R. No. 141314 dated November 15, 2002, affirmed on April 9, 2003). Consequently, BSP-increased interest rate will not dampen their demand for additional loans needed for capital and operating expenditures. They can simply pass on the increase in interest expense to consumers to maintain their 12% allowable profit rate.

In the present case, BSP's latest further hike in already high interest rate will not arrest inflation on goods and services that matter to mass consumers—because it has nothing to do with the

CAUSES of rise in inflation: mainly increase in FOOD prices and TRANSPORT COST.

On inflation on FOOD prices, the substantial increase in September of RICE retail price was caused by concentration of rice supply solely in private traders who seemingly indulged in cartelized hoarding and price manipulation. *The government was helpless in preventing the increase in rice prices* because the BSP representative and other bank officials in the NFA Council apparently slept on their job. *They failed to work for enough NFA funding for its buffer stock or rice reserve inventory, hence NFA had no cheap rice to unload in the market to temper the steep rise in rice prices.*

Scarcity in supply caused inflation on PORK and VEGETABLE prices. Piggeries were decimated by the Asian swine flu (ASF), while vegetable farms were damaged by strong typhoons. Without competing enough supply of pork and vegetables, prices of CHICKEN and FISH also rose. Under these market conditions, BSP can raise its interest rate even higher to, say 30% as in the Asian crisis, but it will still not reduce the high food prices. It will even counteract production and cause higher prices and loan delinquencies.

The higher inflation on TRANSPORT COST is due mainly to increase in fuel and maintenance costs as well as hike in regulated tollway rates. For instance, in the case of diesel oil used as fuel in land and sea passenger and cargo transport, raising interest rate will not affect diesel price and its upward impact or INFLATION on transport cost—because diesel pricing is based on movements of international posted oil prices without regard to level of local interest rate.

CONCLUDING NOTE

In sum, BSP's present high-interest-rate monetary tool against inflation is harmful to the nation's commerce and industry, especially to struggling micro, small, and medium enterprises in the economy—but it is of dubious benefit.

1. Firstly, against INFLATION on non-essential and luxury products, high interest rate is not really beneficial because, while it adversely affects the demand and thereby arrests inflation on these products, there is no need to contain their inflation through burdensome high lending rate—because the generally poor mass consumers themselves can avoid the inflation. As these products are not basic needs, consumers can simply switch to suitable cheap substitutes or forego purchase altogether.

2. Secondly, against INFLATION on basic necessities like power and water, high interest rate on loans of monopoly public service providers has NO diminishing EFFECT on the inelastic demand for these products—precisely because these are basic necessities with unavoidable and stable demand based on need. Therefore, there is no resulting tempered demand from high interest rate that will automatically restrain price increase or INFLATION. Moreover, the rates or prices of basic necessities are REGULATED and not dependent on the level of interest rate.

Accordingly, BSP must discard its present high interest rate against INFLATION and employ instead the better and less painful alternatives to it, as presented in the coming 2nd email.

MARCELO L. TECSON
A CPA and Concerned Citizen

Good Governance Advocate
Author, *Inequality: Economic Tyranny* (2022 Edition)
Author, *Puzzlers: Economic Sting* (published in 2005)

Bonifacio Global City and
San Miguel, Bulacan
November 14, 2023

Cc through separate letters/emails:
Select executive and legislative government officials
Select members of media, academe, and economic society
Select civil society groups and concerned citizens

EVIDENTIARY EXHIBITS

PHILIPPINE DAILY INQUIRER, JANUARY 14, 1998, PAGE B1

Editor ■ CORRIE S. NARISMA, Assistant Editor

EXHIBIT 1

BSP hikes lending rate to ward off speculators

BY DORIS C. DUMLAO

THE BANGKO Sentral ng Pilipinas yesterday raised its overnight lending rate to 16 percent from 15.4 percent to align its rates with this week's uptick in benchmark Treasury bill rates.

ASIAWEEK Magazine
July 31, 1998, Page 54

BANK RATES AND CURRENCY MOVEMENTS

	PRIME LENDING	TIME DEPOSIT RATES (PERCENT PER YEAR)				RISE/FA
	last week	1 month	3 mo.	6 mo.	12 mo.	6 mo.
HK$	10.00	7.19	7.94	9.28	10.00	---
S$	7.50	5.25	5.25	5.25	5.38	+2.2
Ringgit	12.10	10.30	10.30	10.30	10.30	+1.7
Peso	18.00	13.25	13.25	13.25	13.25	-0.7
Baht	15.50	---	12.00	12.00	12.75	+27.1
Rupiah	65.00	51.00	42.00	31.00	31.00	-39.1
Won	11.50	7.00	7.00	7.00	9.00	+25.5
NT$	8.10	6.40	6.50	6.40	6.50	-1.5
NZ$	12.55	6.96	7.06	7.25	7.31	-10.6
US$	8.50	5.53	5.56	5.62	5.68	

Sources: Standard Chartered Bank, Hong Kong; Asiaweek Research. *HK$ is pegged to the greenback with a narrow trading

54 Indonesian prime lending rate: 65%   ASIAWEEK JULY 31.

EXHIBIT 3

britannica

Coming Soon !

100 Years with Nobel Laureates

100 articles by 100 laureates exclusively for Encyclopaedia Britannica.

Encyclopaedia Britannica 2002 Deluxe Edition CD-ROM (for Windows)

Encyclopaedia Britannica 2002 Deluxe Edition CD-

Bad debts loom large over Asian banks

November 1, 2001

Asian economies' inability of to tackle bad debts or non-performing loans (NPLs) may affect their banking system and economic growth for years to come. This was revealed by leading financial consultancy, Ernst & Young after surveying eight countries – Japan, China, Taiwan, South Korea, Thailand, Malaysia, Indonesia, and the Philippines. The final report of the survey, Nonperforming Loan Report: Asia 2002, is expected to be out by January 2002.

Britannica.com | Australia |

Nobel Prize

A 100 ye

Timeline

Total Outstanding Non Performing Loans: Reported Vs. Estimated Levels

	Reported	Estimated
Indonesia	18.5%	60%
Thailand	12.5%	45%
China	28%	40%
Philippines	16.6%	32%
Japan	16.3%	27%
Malaysia	11.5%	25%
South Korean	9.5%	21%
Taiwan	6.5%	25%

WEDNESDAY, JANUARY 13, 1999

PHILIPPINE DAILY INQUIRER

International BUSINESS

STILL NO SOLUTION

Central bankers share gripes on speculation

HONG KONG—Central bankers from around the globe have found no immediate solution to a question that has troubled Asian leaders for nearly two years: How to control currency speculators.

The Swiss-based organization, which acts as a clearing house for the world's central banks, organized the meeting of the 17 monetary chiefs at its Hong Kong office.

US Federal Reserve chair Alan Greenspan attended the meeting as part of his tour through Asia.

EXHIBIT 6

ALAN Greenspan, right, chair of the US Federal Reserve, rushes to a meeting in Hong Kong with international central bankers to discuss the global economy, and in particular financial developments in Asia. The man on left is unidentified. AP

EVIDENTIARY EXHIBIT

EXHIBIT 7

Quezon City
April 1, 1998

'98 APR 17 P12:13

FOR: H. E. President Fidel V. Ramos
        BSP Governor Gabriel Singson
        BSP Monetary Board Members
        Other Government Officials Concerned
        Others Adversely Affected By Economic Crisis

SUBJECT: The Government Must Stop Plight Of Borrowers of One Trillion Pesos Loans Not
           Usable In Dollar Speculation, Yet Unjustly Subjected To High Interest Rates

Implementation ERROR in high interest rates contributed immensely to the relatively poor performance of the present administration in its last year and the growing disenchantment of many Filipinos, especially the innocent victims of high interest rates. Indiscriminate high lending rates that miss their targets, not peso devaluation, drove the economy to gridlock.

XXXX   10

(a) CHANGE HIGH INTEREST RATES TO HIGH LOAN REPAYMENT RATES

As discussed, it is the increase in periodic loan payments that actually tightens money supply. BSP stimulated this increase in loan payments INDIRECTLY through high interest rates. BSP can stimulate this increase DIRECTLY by inducing or requiring all borrowers to increase their periodic loan payments equivalent to the needed increase in interest rates. Given no option except to choose between high loan repayment rates and high interest rates, the borrowers will choose high loan repayment rates. XXXX

(b) OTHER ALTERNATIVES TO HIGH INTEREST RATES

The ideal alternative is a solution that will attack the problem directly, that is, as the possible main sources of borrowed funds usable in dollar speculation are new loans, it should curtail new loans only. However, this is still counter-productive because most new loans may be used for legitimate investments and not in dollar speculation. A more ideal alternative then is to sort out loans that can used for dollar speculation, if this can be practically done, or go straight to dollar purchases and try to identify those which can be for speculative purposes only. BSP may require supporting documents, such as proof of existing dollar obligations, for substantial dollar purchases done through the banking system, so that those without actual foreign obligations may be construed as intended for dollar speculation. Anyway, it is up to BSP to find viable alternative measures. Just because none are found yet does not mean that it should stick to and maintain this highly disastrous high interest rate solution. XXXX

MARCELO L. TECSON

EXHIBIT 9

Bangko Sentral ng Pilipinas

MAYNILA, PILIPINAS

OFFICE OF THE GOVERNOR

CIRCULAR NO. 138
Series of 1997

SUBJECT: **Further Amendment of Section 2 of
CB Circular No. 1389, as Amended**

Pursuant to Monetary Board Resolution No. 995, dated July 30, 1997, Section 2 of Central Bank Circular No. 1389, as amended, is further amended to read as follows:

"Section 2. Sales of Foreign Exchange by AABs. AABs may sell foreign exchange to residents (including the Government, its political subdivisions/instrumentalities and government-owned and -controlled corporations), for any non-trade purpose, without need of prior Bangko Sentral ng Pilipinas (BSP) approval, provided that:

a)   for sales of foreign exchange exceeding US$25,000.00, the AAB shall require a written notarized application and supporting documents from the purchaser of the foreign exchange; and

b)   for sales of foreign exchange not exceeding US$25,000.00, the AAB shall require a written application only.

The written application required under b) shall be in accordance with the attached format.

AABs shall see to it that this limit on the sale of foreign exchange for a non-trade purpose is not breached by the splitting of a foreign exchange purchase into smaller amounts so as to make it appear that the purchase does not violate the prescribed limit.

There is deemed to be a splitting of a foreign exchange purchase within the prohibition of this Circular if a Bank sells foreign exchange for a non-trade purpose to any one purchaser, within a fifteen banking day period, in such individual amounts which, when combined, exceed $25,000.00.

The AAB shall report all sales covered by this section under FED I using the appropriate transaction codes.

For sales of foreign exchange for payment of obligations that are foreign loan- or foreign investment-related, the AAB shall require purchaser's presentation of proof of BSP approval and/or registration for each loan or investment, whenever required by existing rules."

This Circular shall take effect immediately.

For the Monetary Board:

GABRIEL C. SINGSON
Governor

31 July 1997

ITAGUYOD ANG PHILIPPINES 2000   MAG-IMPOK SA BANGKO

EXHIBIT 10

PHILIPPINE DAILY INQUIRER

B8 MONDAY, AUGUST 28, 2000

BUSINESS

BSP CRACKDOWN

20 banks fined ₱1.2M for peso speculation

BY CLARISSA S. BATINO

THE BANGKO Sentral ng Pilipinas has slapped P1.2 million worth of fines against 20 foreign and local banks and their affiliates for violating the government's reportorial requirements and speculating against the peso.

The policy-making Monetary Board refused to divulge the names of these institutions.

BSP Governor Rafael Buenaventura warned of severe sanctions for second-time offenders.

"We will tell them that if they repeat these violations, their licenses would be suspended for three months to a year and even their bank officers would be suspended," Buenaventura told reporters.

The central bank last week accused eight banks of bringing down the peso's value against the US dollar by speculating against the local currency between May and June this year.

A person familiar with the situation told reporters that among the banks in the BSP's list were Standard Chartered Bank, HSBC Holdings Inc., Deutsche Bank AG, Citibank NA, ING Bank and Equitable PCI-Bank.

These banks allegedly brought down the peso's value from 41 to a dollar in April to 43.74 in late May. They were said to have speculated against the local currency again in late June, which caused the peso to fall to 45.15 in mid-July.

The central bank said these banks ⌐

EXHIBIT 11

PHILIPPINE DAILY INQUIRER   FRIDAY, AUGUST 10, 2001   ★★   50 PAGES   5 !

9 big banks fined for $ speculation

Macapagal issues strong warning

By Clarissa S. Batino

THE BANGKO Sentral ng Pilipinas yesterday slapped fines on nine big banks for violating foreign exchange regulations after President Macapagal-Arroyo warned currency speculators to beware.

In an unprecedented move, the BSP identified the three foreign and six local banks found speculating against the peso from June to July when the local currency slumped to as low as P54 against the US dollar.

The foreign banks penalized by the BSP were Citibank, P210,000; Hong Kong Shanghai Banking Corp., P90,000; and Standard Chartered Bank, P30,000.

The local banks meted out fines were Banco de Oro, P3,210,000; Export and Industry Bank, P720,000; Bank of the Philippine

EXHIBIT 12

MANILA BULLETIN
THE NATION'S LEADING NEWSPAPER
101 Years of Service to the Nation
BUSINESS
CLASSIFIED ADS

SATURDAY, AUGUST 11, 2001 ● http://www.mb.com.ph   B-1

Peso rebounds to ₱51.85
from ₱53.05 to dollar

By FIL C. SIONIL

The peso traded at a wider range yesterday from an intra-day low of ₱52.95 to an intra-day high of ₱51.70, the highest intra-day gain in two months this year.

At the end of the trading at the Philippine Dealing System, the peso closed at ₱51.85, with the weighted average rate setting at ₱52.322, a 76.3 centavos gain from last Thursday's ₱53.085 to a dollar.

The peso's recovery came after President Arroyo urged the Bangko Sentral to bring down the exchange rate to ₱50 or lower to the dollar by the end of the year.

Total volume that changed hands at the PDS hit $151.7 million, the largest volume ever recorded two weeks on apparent unloading of dollars by a number of banks.

BSP Governor Rafael B. Buenaventura said the recovery of the peso back to ₱51 levels was "reflective of the market." "The (peso-dollar) rates should be in the lower ₱50s rather the higher ₱50s," Buenaventura said, adding that "the peso (rate) will always be market determined."

A currency dealer of a local bank admitted that the peso appreciation was largely driven by the fierce warning of the monetary authorities to pursue speculators.

"On fear that the BSP really means business, banks, who are mostly long in dollars started to unload, causing a remarkable recovery of the peso," a currency dealer of a domestic bank said.

A dealer of another bank said the recovery of the peso will be sustained next week.

Last Thursday, the Monetary Board, the policy-making body of the BSP, fined nine banks — three foreign and six domestic — for various violations of foreign exchange rules and regulations.

Fined were Citibank, Standard Chartered Bank, Hong Kong Shanghai Banking Corp., Equitable-PCI Bank, Banco de Oro, United Coconut Planters Bank, Bank of the Philippine Islands, China Banking Corporation and Export and Industry Bank.

9

LOVE LETTER TO FILIPINOS - By David H. Harwell, PhD – posted by Rodney Jaleco – Nov. 16, 2023 - Facebook

A sentimental open letter from an American teacher to the Filipino people (Pls. take time to read this)
LOVE LETTER TO FILIPINOS
By David H. Harwell, PhD
I am writing to thank Filipinos for the way you have treated me here, and to pass on a lesson I learned

from observing the differences between your culture and mine over the years.

I am an expatriate worker. I refer to myself as an OAW, an overseas American worker, as a bad joke. The work I do involves a lot of traveling and changing locations, and I do it alone, without family. I have been in 21 countries now, not including my own. It was fun at first. Now, many years later, I am getting tired. The Philippines remains my favorite country of all, though, and I'd like to tell you why before I have to go away again.

I have lived for short periods here, traveled here, and have family and friends here. My own family of origin in the United States is like that of many Americans—not much of a family. Americans do not stay very close to their families, geographically or emotionally, and that is a major mistake. I have long been looking for a home and a family, and the Philippines is the only place I have lived where people honestly seem to understand how important their families are.

I am American and hard-headed. I am a teacher, but it takes me a long time to learn some things. But I've been trying, and your culture has been patient in trying to teach me.

In the countries where I've lived and worked, all over the Middle East and Asia, it is Filipinos who do all the work and make everything happen. When I am working in a new company abroad, I seek out the Filipino staff when I need help getting something done, and done right. Your international reputation as employees is that you work hard, don't complain, and are very capable. If all the Filipinos were to go home from the Middle East, the world would stop. Oil is the lifeblood of the world, but without Filipinos, the oil will not come from the ground, it will not be loaded onto the ships, and the ships will not sail. The offices that make the deals and collect the payments will not even open in the morning. The schools will not have teachers, and, of course, the hospitals will have no staff.

What I have seen, that many of you have not seen, is how your family members, the ones who are overseas Filipino workers, do not tell you much about how hard their lives actually are. OFWs are very often mistreated in other countries, at work and in their personal lives. You probably have not heard much about how they do all the work but are severely underpaid, because they know that the money they are earning must be sent home to you, who depend on them. The OFWs are very strong people, perhaps the strongest I have ever seen. They have their pictures taken in front of nice shops and locations to post on Facebook so that you won't worry about them. But every Pinoy I have ever met abroad misses his/her family very, very much.

I often pity those of you who go to America. You see pictures of their houses and cars, but not what it took to get those things. We have nice things, too many things, in America, but we take on an incredible debt to get them, and the debt is lifelong. America's economy is based on debt. Very rarely is a house, car, nice piece of clothing, electronic appliance, and often even food, paid for. We get them with credit, and this debt will take all of our lifetime to pay. That burden is true for anyone in America—the OFWs, those who are married to Americans, and the Americans themselves.

Most of us allow the American Dream to become the American Trap. Some of you who go there make it back home, but you give up most of your lives before you do. Some of you who go there learn the very bad American habits of wanting too many things in your hands, and the result is that you live only to work, instead of working only to live. The things we own actually own us. That is the great mistake we Americans make in our lives. We live only to work, and we work only to buy more things that we don't need. We lose our lives in the process.

I have sometimes tried to explain it like this: In America, our hands are full, but our hearts are empty.

You have many problems here, I understand that. Americans worry about having new cars, Filipinos worry about having enough food to eat. That's an enormous difference. But do not envy us, because we should learn something from you. What I see is that even when your hands are empty, your hearts remain full.

I have many privileges in the countries where I work, because I am an expat. I do not deserve these things, but I have them. However, in every country I visit, I see that you are there also, taking care of your families, friends, bosses, and coworkers first, and yourselves last. And you have always taken care of me, in this country and in every other place where I have been.

These are places where I have been very alone, very tired, very hungry, and very worried, but there have always been Filipinos in my offices, in the shops, in the restaurants, in the hospitals, everywhere, who smile at and take good care of me. I always try to let you know that I have lived and traveled in the Philippines and how much I like your country. I know that behind those smiles of yours, here and abroad, are many worries and problems.

Please know that at least one of us expats has seen what you do for others and understands that you have a story behind your smiles. Know that at least one of us admires you, respects you, and thanks you for your sacrifices. Salamat po. Ingat lagi. Mahal ko kayong lahat.

David H. Harwell, PhD, is a former professor and assistant dean in the United States who now travels and works abroad designing language training programs. He is a published author and a son of a retired news editor.

Feel free to pass along

....

10
PUNLA PARA SA BAYAN – VICTORIA SMITH GROUP – OCT. 28, 2023

UPDATED & REVISED MEMORANDUM OF FACTS & EVIDENCE PROVING THE SYSTEMATIC RIGGING OF THE 2022 PHILIPPINE NATIONAL AND LOCAL ELECTIONS (NLE)

By: Victoria Grageda-Smith for PUNLA Para Sa Bayan

This is a memorandum of facts and evidence that proves the systematic rigging of the 2022 Philippine National and Local Elections (NLE) that favored the Marcos-Duterte "win."

The evidence suggests, among others, that the Commission on Elections (COMELEC), Smartmatic (with the cooperation of the three Telcos: Globe, Smart, and Dito), F2 Logistics, and the Marcos-Duterte ticket possessed the (1) MOTIVE, (2) MEANS, and (3) OPPORTUNITY to commit electoral fraud.

While it may be argued that no single fact or proof cited below could be sufficient, alone, to indubitably prove the systematic rigging of the 2022 NLE and may only constitute circumstantial evidence, it is submitted that all such circumstantial evidence, taken together, amounts to a greater than a preponderance of evidence of electoral fraud.

Above all, it is submitted that, above and beyond the 2022 NLE having been systematically rigged as to adequately prove electoral fraud sufficient to prove a failure of elections under election law, the whole 2022 NLE is null and void by virtue, alone, of it having been conducted in an unlawful manner or through a system that did not follow or conform to, or was in gross violation of law. For this reason, it is also submitted that there is no need to file a petition for a declaration of a failure of elections, for this does not fall under the usual electoral fraud intended or provided for by law for such a declaration.

The inherently illegal nature of the 2022 NLE is in a class by itself and, considering the clear bias that the current Philippine Supreme Court (SC) has displayed for the illegitimate Marcos-Duterte government, is one that does not need to be recognized by the SC but, rather, must be acted upon by the Filipino people themselves through a new People Power Revolution to oust the illegitimate government and all its puppets. This is the only solution, realistically and philosophically, to the problem of an illegitimate government.

1. MOTIVE to commit electoral fraud.

There is considerable motive for the Marcoses and Dutertes to win at all costs during the 2022 Philippine elections and, likewise, for their cronies, puppets, and appointees, such as the COMELEC Commissioners, to help install and keep them in power.

The following show why the Marcoses and the Dutertes needed to win the 2022 elections and how they did it unlawfully:

1.1. The Marcos-Duterte Conspiracy. The Marcoses and the Dutertes have been, and are a team. Their close cooperative workings may even qualify them as a syndicate—a group that conspires to gain and maintain political and economic power through their government positions. They are complicit in what they do, for they are conspirators in one shared goal: keeping themselves in power for their self-interests.

1.1.a. Former president Rodrigo Duterte publicly admitted it was the Marcoses who had funded his presidential campaign. (Proof: a publicly available video)

1.1.b. On August 7, 2016, President Rodrigo Duterte gave the order that allowed the burial of former President Ferdinand Marcos, Sr. at the Libingan ng mga Bayani despite the former dictator's grave sins against the country and the Filipino people, ignoring massive public protest against such action.

1.1.c. Rodrigo Duterte brazenly and arbitrarily ignored grave conflicts of interest in the appointments of people and awarding of contracts crucial to the 2022 NLE that clearly show motive to ensure the victory of his daughter, Sara Duterte, and Ferdinand Marcos, Jr.

1.1.c.i. The former president Duterte appointed most of the members of the SC, including the COMELEC. Both agencies show their clear bias for the Marcoses and Dutertes by issuing decisions favorable to the political tandem, ensuring the Marcoses' return to political power in the Philippines while keeping the Dutertes in power.

1.1.c.ii. Among other decisions favorable to the Marcoses, the SC dismissed the remaining ill-gotten wealth cases against the Marcoses and removed the prison term imposed by the Philippine Court of Appeals (CA) on Marcos, Jr. for his conviction for tax evasion.

1.1.c.iii. Among other decisions favorable to the Marcoses, the COMELEC allowed Marcos, Jr.'s presidential candidacy despite the latter having been convicted of the crime of tax evasion, for which he was penalized with a huge fine and would have gone to seven (7) years in prison had the SC not removed the prison term of his punishment. Likewise relevant is the fact that COMELEC Chair George Garcia is none other than Marcos, Jr.'s former lawyer.

1.1.c.iv. COMELEC awarded F2 Logistics the contract to handle and transport all election paraphernalia (inclusive of ballots, ballot boxes, and Vote Counting Machines [VCMs]) despite strong objections based on conflict of interest. The conflict of interest arose out of the fact that F2 Logistics is owned by well-known Marcos and Duterte friend and supporter, Dennis Uy. (Proofs, among others, of such alliance are the many social media pictures showing Uy partying and meeting with the Marcoses and Dutertes; proofs of the contracts awarded in favor of F2 Logistics and Smartmatic; corporate documents showing Uy's ownership or F2 Logistics, including his interest in Smartmatic; news articles)

1.1.c.v. COMELEC awarded the contract to provide the Automated Election System (AES) to Smartmatic (in which Dennis Uy is said to also have an interest), despite public criticisms (even coming from Marcos, Jr. himself in 2016) and protests against Smartmatic as a world-renowned tool for election cheating. (Proof, among others: a video recording of Marcos, Jr. declaring in 2016 that Smartmatic only exists as a tool for election cheating; news articles about Smartmatic's involvement with electoral fraud in several countries from where it had subsequently been banned)

1.1.d. Rodrigo Duterte's daughter, Sara, ran as a team with Ferdinand Marcos, Jr. as the latter's vice-presidential candidate in the 2022 NLE. The electoral fraud described hereunder likewise benefited her by illegitimately installing her as vice-president, alongside Marcos, Jr. as president.

1.1.e. In an affidavit dated September 21, 2023, Atty. Glenn Chong stated that the wife of then-presidential candidate Marcos, Jr., Liza Araneta Marcos, had arranged to meet before the elections with the president of the AES provider, Smartmatic, in violation of election law and Smartmatic's "Contract for the Procurement of Secure Electronic Services for the 2022 NLE Election Results" (SETS contract) with the COMELEC.

1.2. The High Stakes for the Marcos Clan and Marcos, Jr.'s Power, as Illegitimate President, to Overturn Judicial Decisions Against Him and His Clan. As president, Marcos, Jr. could defeat, overturn, and/or render moot and academic the following nine (9) outstanding judicial decisions, domestic and international, against him and his family, including ensuring that his mother, Imelda Marcos; his sister, Imee Marcos; and himself remain safe from imprisonment. Some of these things have already come to pass.

The following judicial decisions from various countries describe the high stakes for the Marcoses that provided them with the mandatory motivation to win the 2022 NLE:

1.2.a. In 2019, the Sandiganbayan ordered the forfeiture & seizure of $24M worth of that Marcos painting collection as 'ill-gotten wealth.' (Estate of Marcos v. Republic)

1.2.b. In 2018, the Sandiganbayan convicted Imelda Marcos of 7 counts of graft and sentenced her bet. 6-11 yrs per count of illegally funneling $200M to Swiss foundations in the '70s as Metropolitan Manila governor. (People v. Imelda Marcos).

1.2.c. In 2017, the Philippine SC upheld the 2014 Sandiganbayan decision ordering the forfeiture of Marcos jewelry as ill-gotten wealth. (Estate of Marcos v. Republic)

1.2.d. In 2012, the 9th Circuit U.S. Court of Appeals (Hawaii) penalized Imelda Marcos & Ferdinand 'BongBong' Marcos II as co-executors and co-administrators of the Marcos Estate with a $353.6 million fine for contempt of court (for disobeying the court order not to move or transfer Marcos assets). (In Re Estate of Marcos Human Rights Litigation)

1.2.e. In 2011, the Supreme Court of Honolulu affirmed its 1998 decision upholding the 1996 9th Circuit Court of Honolulu decision that upheld the 1994 ($1.2B award) and 1995 (extra $766M exemplary damages award) District Court awards in the total amount of $2B judgment against the Marcos estate under the 'command responsibility' principle of the Alien Tort Claims Act of 1789 in favor of Filipino human rights violations victims under a guilty verdict in the 1992 trial and approved execution against Marcos properties in the U.S. (In Re Estate of Marcos Human Rights Litigation)

1.2.f. In 2009, the Philippine SC upheld the 1997 CA decision imposing tax liabilities on the Marcos estate (now more than P203B, inclusive of penalties & interest). (Republic v. Marcos, Jr.)

1.2.g. In 2001, the Philippine SC affirmed the 1997 CA decision that modified the 1995 ruling of the Quezon City Regional Trial Court (RTC) that found

Ferdinand "Bongbong" R. Marcos Jr. guilty of eight counts of violations of the National Internal Revenue Code (NIRC) of 1977. (Marcos II v. Court of Appeals)

1.2.h. In 2000, the Hawaii court found against the Marcos Estate in favor of the estate of Rogelio Roxas and the Golden Buddha Corporation, awarding $20 million to the heirs of Roxas. (Roxas v. Marcos)

1.2.i. In 1992, the District Court of Honolulu, Hawaii in Trajano v. Marcos found Imee Marcos-Manotoc civilly liable for the death of Archimedes Trajano and ordered her to pay the Trajano family $4.16 million in damages (a decision that a Philippine court refused to acknowledge and enforce).

1.3. Marcos, Jr.'s Power, as Illegitimate President, to Reverse the Recovery of the Marcoses' Ill-Gotten Wealth. As president, Ferdinand Marcos, Jr. could recover his family's confiscated ill-gotten wealth, as already proven by the following:

1.3.a. The Philippine SC resolved to return the Php 1.5 billion (which was in the name of Marcos cronies) that used to be in the custody of the Philippine Commission on Good Government (PCGG).

1.3.b. There remain Php 2.5 billion under the control of the PCGG that are now vulnerable to likewise being recovered by the Marcoses under Marcos Jr. as president.

1.4. Marcos, Jr.'s Power, as Illegitimate President, to Enable His Clan and Cronies to Amass More Ill-Gotten Wealth. As president, Ferdinand Marcos, Jr. could enable his family and their cronies and puppets to amass more ill-gotten wealth, as already demonstrated by the following:

1.4.a. The Marcos-Duterte government facilitated the speedy passage of the Maharlika Investment Fund (MIF; a publicly-known brainchild of Marcos, Jr.) bill into law.

1.4.b. The MIF draws upon the funds of Philippine government banks: the Development Bank of the Philippines (DBP), Land Bank of the Philippines (LBP), and Central Bank of the Philippines (CBP).

1.4.c. Based on the historical behavior of the Marcos family, as shown by acts of the Marcos, Sr. regime exploiting the Philippine government banks as the Marcos family's personal piggy banks (such as the Philippine National Bank), it is reasonable to expect that the Marcoses will do the same through the MIF, among other means.

1.4.d. The above is supported by the recent suspension by Marcos, Jr. of the MIF law—yet, tellingly, only after the DBP and LBP paid a total of Php seventy-five (75) billion of their capital contributions to the fund. This means such amounts are now under the complete control of the Marcos-Duterte government without any responsibility to fulfill the avowed goals of such fund nor accountability for the handling, location, and safekeeping of the Php 75B already paid by the DBP and LBP.

1.4. e. Marcos, Jr. actively seeks to gain control of the most resource-rich sources of assets of the Philippines, such as the Government Service Insurance System (GSIS) fund. He also named himself Secretary of Agriculture, which thereby gave him access to one of the biggest, if not the biggest wealth-generating industry in the Philippines.

1.4.f. The Marcos-Duterte government has arbitrarily appropriated for itself "Confidential" and "Intelligence" funds (CIFs) in the billions of pesos to spend as it pleases, without legal need to account to the Filipino people for how it spends or allocates such funds.

2. MEANS to commit electoral fraud.

The COMELEC, in complicity with Smartmatic (and, probably, in conjunction with the Telcos Globe, Smart, and Dito), F2 Logistics, and the Marcos-Duterte ticket had ample means, methods, or tools to systematically rig the 2022 NLE to favor a Marcos-Duterte "win."

2.1. The Nature of AES Technology. The nature of the AES technology is in the form of a programmable, re-programmable, and pre-programmable set of computer instructions that could be placed, inserted, introduced, and /or changed, amended, and revised in all of the units and components of the AES, such as the AES software and hardware (including VCMs); SD Cards, and the Telco Exchange described below. (Proof, among others: the TNTrio's and other IT experts' opinions)

2.2. The Original AES End-to-End Transmission Path. On March 22, 2022, the COMELEC presented to the Filipino people, and the Filipino people approved and agreed to the "End-to-End Path Transmission" (hereinafter called the "Protocol") of the 2022 ERs through the AES, which, among others, specified that the method of transmission of the ERs by the precinct VCMs) to the municipality, provincial, national, and COMELEC Servers would be conducted in accordance with the ladderized transmission system mandated by law (Republic Act 9369 and COMELEC Resolution No. 10754) and the SETS contract between COMELEC and Smartmatic.

2.3. COMELEC's Unlawful Use of Secret and Illegal Private IP Addresses. In March 2023, the COMELEC published raw files on its website showing the transmissions of ERs to the COMELEC Transparency Server (TS). Such raw files showed the stunning use of private IP addresses to transmit ERs.

2.3.a. Most of the ERs transmitted to the COMELEC TS came only from illegal private IP addresses. (Proof, among others: COMELEC website raw files and data; the admissions of COMELEC Chair Garcia and a COMELEC lawyer-spokesperson on COMELEC's use of a private network and IP addresses in ER transmissions)

2.3.b. Such use of private IP addresses was unlawful and, therefore, such private IP addresses were illegal, based on the Protocol because the Protocol was premised on the use of the internet by the Telcos to transmit ERs from the VCMs to the municipality, provincial, national, and COMELEC Servers, which necessarily meant by the way the technology works that only public IP addresses could and should have been used.

2.4. COMELEC's Unlawful Use of a Secret Private Network called the "Telco Exchange." During the Senate COMELEC Budget Committee hearing on September 14, 2023, COMELEC Chair George Garcia—for the first time, and after more than a year of the 2022 elections, and only after the Truth and Transparency Trio composed of Eliseo Rio, Jr., Augusto Lagman, and Frank Ysaac (TNTrio) exposed the COMELEC's use of illegal private IP addresses, and in a vain attempt to explain the use of illegal private IP addresses—admitted to having created and utilized a wholly private network that it called the "Telco Exchange" for the transmission of ERs during the 2022 NLE.

2.4.a. Garcia presented a diagram that demonstrated how this previously secret Telco Exchange operated, to wit:

2.4.a.i. The VCMs transmitted their ERs directly to the Telco Exchange, which, then, transmitted such ERs to the municipal boards of canvassers and the COMELEC Transparency and Central Servers.

2.4.a.ii. The municipal boards of canvassers then sent each of their certificates of canvass back to the Telco Exchange, which, then, sent the data to the provincial, district, and national boards of canvassers, respectively and consecutively.

2.4.a.iii. Such provincial, district, and national boards of canvassers, respectively and consecutively, then sent their certificates of canvass back to the Telco Exchange.

2.4.a.iv. Such back-and-forth transmissions between the Telco Exchange are not the same as the ladderized transmissions described and mandated by the Protocol and by law (Republic Act 9369 and COMELEC Resolution No. 10754) and contract (SETS)

2.4.b. The Telco Exchange was a gross violation of both law and contract because:

2.4.b.i. It did not follow the ladderized ER transmissions specified and mandated by the Protocol, law (Republic Act 9369 and COMELEC Resolution No. 10754) and contract (SETS).

2.4.b.ii. The Telco Exchange constituted a single point Man-in-the-Middle (MITM) device that rendered the Philippine AES vulnerable to being a single point of failure that, thereby, likewise did not conform to the best practices for automated election systems. (Proofs: the various expert opinion statements of Eliseo Rio, Jr. and the ICT Leaders for Good Governance Manifesto and Technology Explainer)

2.4.b.iii. The Telco Exchange, being a Man-in-the-Middle (MITM) device, was equivalent to the "meet-me-room" and "queue server" that the COMELEC, in the aftermath of previous elections, was expressly prohibited by Congress from using again. The difference in terminology is irrelevant, for the way the Telco Exchange as a Man-in-the-Middle (MITM) device, the "meet-me-room," and "queue server" worked—which was to introduce an external, unknown, secret, and unapproved device to transmit ERs—was in gross violation of election law.

2.4.c. The COMELEC, through its Telco Exchange diagram and description, failed to explain, in terms that made sense to the way technology works, the use of only one private IP address (192.168.0.2) in transmitting ERs from 20,300 VCMs and how such single private IP address (192.168.0.2) could have sent 39,000 ERs that registered 20M+ votes within only the first hour after voting closed (which made the Marcos-Duterte triumph a fait accompli). (Proofs, among others: COMELEC TS Reception Log, website raw files and data, COMELEC's Telco Exchange diagram, and the Sept. 14, 2023 Senate COMELEC Budget hearing video)

2.4.c.i. While the use of one private IP address (192.168.0.2) to transmit the ERs of 20,300 VCMs is theoretically technically possible under what COMELEC Commissioner Nelson Celis (another appointee of Marcos, Jr.) declared during the September 14, 2023 Senate COMELEC Budget hearing as having part of the design of the Telco Exchange—namely, a network address translation (NAT) system—such an allegation does not make sense because:

2.4.c.i.1. There are 17M private IP addresses available and, therefore, no inadequacy of private IP addresses that the COMELEC could have accessed and used—instead of limiting itself to just a single private IP address, namely, illegal private IP Address 192.168.0.2.

2.4.c.i.2. A NAT is used to translate several private IP addresses into a single public IP address, not the other way around—meaning, not to translate several private IP addresses into just one private IP address.

2.4.c.i.3. If what the COMELEC alleges is true—that it connected all the VCMs within a wholly private network—one would not need a NAT.

2.4.c.ii. COMELEC's failure and continued failure to present the telco call data records (CDRs) of the 20,300 VCMs strongly suggest that the ERs did not come from 20,300 VCMs but, rather, from a single MITM device (which is, by the way, the very nature of the Telco Exchange) that was assigned the single private IP Address 196.168.0.2.

2.4.c.iii. Paragraph 2.4.c.ii above strongly suggests that the Telco Exchange itself was the MITM device that had fed preprogrammed ERs into the AES. In other words, since COMELEC, Smartmatic, and the Telcos were integral partners in the creation of the Telco Exchange, it follows that COMELEC, Smartmatic, and the Telcos were complicit in the systematic rigging of the 2022 NLE.

2.4.d. During the September 14, 2023 Senate COMELEC Budget hearing, Chair Garcia identified Globe as the telco that had assigned private illegal IP Address 192.168.0.2 to 20,300 VCMs for the transmission of their ERs. However, this statement is not supported by the Telco records that COMELEC itself chose to publish on its website.

2.4.d.i. Private illegal IP address 192.168.0.2 does not appear at all in any of the Globe CDRs that COMELEC had published on its website. Such Globe CDRs are also dubious because they are incomplete (and, therefore, indicative of having been selectively chosen) and, on their face, clearly show themselves as having been modified (and, therefore, indicative of being manufactured, not true records).

2.4.d.ii. Neither does such private illegal IP Address 192.168.0.2 appear in any of the partial and selected Smart records that COMELEC published on its website. Such Smart records likewise do not appear to be CDRs at all because they lack the MSISDN (mobile number) of the devices that had supposedly transmitted the ERs.

2.4.d.iii. It also bears noting that COMELEC has not mentioned nor offered to publish or has published the CDRs of the third Telco, Dito—which was owned before and during the NLE by the same Dennis Uy who is a close friend and supporter of both the Marcoses and Dutertes and also owns F2 Logistics, the entity to which COMELEC had awarded the contract to provide AES materials and their transportation, inclusive of ballot boxes and VCMs.

2.5. The Total Failure of the 2022 AES Integrity and Verification Process. The following show that system integrity verification and certification process for the AES was a total failure and, therefore, the results of the NLE conducted through such AES could not be trusted:

2.5.a. There was a complete absence of transparency in the system source code and hash code generation and verification.

2.5.a.i. None of the election stakeholders were present or were invited to witness and verify the system source code and hash code generation.

2.5.a.ii. The SD Card configuration by Smartmatic and the COMELEC was performed secretly. It was never shown publicly; nor was its integrity verified and certified by the election stakeholders, watchdogs, or anyone outside of COMELEC and Smartmatic.

2.5.a.iii. Aside from the system hash code generation for one (1) demonstration VCM (demo VCM), no other hash codes were shared by the COMELEC with the public.

2.5.b. There were hash code discrepancies that strongly suggest that the source code in the VCM SD Cards was edited or tampered with.

2.5.b.i. Every computer program generates a source code and its software fingerprint, the hash code, such that if the hash code later turns out to be different, then it means the source code was edited or tampered with.

2.5.b.ii. On February 22, 2022, the COMELEC publicly presented and ran a demo VCM that generated a particular hash code.

2.5.b.iii. On March 22, 2022, during the COMELEC public presentation of how the AES would work, NAMFREL noticed that the hash code shown was different from the one generated on February 22, 2022, and called everyone's, including the COMELEC's attention thereto.

2.5.b.iv. The COMELEC dismissed the issue as a mere typo error, ignoring the fact that hash codes are generated automatically by the system, not manually typed.

2.5.b.v. Based on paragraphs 2.5.b.ii, 2.5.b.iii, and 2.5.b.iv above, the logical conclusion is that the information or program fed into the VCMs through SD Cards on election day, May 9, 2022, was edited or tampered with since the hash code generation and revelation conducted by COMELEC on February 22, 2022.

2.5.c. Election watchdogs refused to verify the integrity of the ballots delivered to Diamond Hotel by F2 Logistics for Random Manual Audit because COMELEC could not account for the integrity of the ballot boxes' chain of custody. Moreover, the ballot boxes were not in a secure form, as they were merely unsealed and flimsy cardboard boxes.

2.6. Proofs of Preprogramming. The COMELEC Transparency Server (TS) appeared to have already known what ERs the VCMs would transmit even before the VCMs transmitted them, thus further supporting that preprogrammed ERs constituted a major role in the systematic rigging of the NLE.

2.6.a. There are time discrepancies between when the TS received the ERs and when the precinct VCMs transmitted the ERs as shown by time-stamped ER receipts showing that the TS received the ERs even before the VCMs transmitted them—sometimes, by as much as more than one hour.

2.6.b. Moreover, the Globe and Smart documents that COMELEC published on its website show that several VCMs unlawfully transmitted ERs as early as the day before election day and seven (7) hours before voting had legally closed.

2.6.c. The ERs shown by the TS and the printed ER receipts of election watchdogs and party-list candidates show the same data, while the time transmissions are different, strongly suggesting that the ERs were pre-programmed to reflect the same ER data (since the TS already knew what ER data to register even before the precinct VCMs transmitted the ER data).

2.6.c.i. Pre-programming involves, precisely, the intentional programming and feeding of the same data everywhere to ensure consistent data registration and results when cross-checked. In other words, the consistency of ER data everywhere is, by itself, a manifestation of pre-programming rather than automatic integrity of election results.

2.6.c.ii. Given paragraph 2.6.c.i above, it is not a rebuttal or proof against accusations of electoral fraud, as the COMELEC tries to argue, that the same election-related data could be found everywhere, such as in ballots (can easily be faked), audit logs (can easily be manipulated by technology), SD Cards, (can be easily be pre-programmed, especially since their configuration was kept highly secret by COMELEC and Smartmatic), Reception Log (part of the stream of information that could reasonably be assumed as pre-programmed), and the ER receipts of election watchdogs PPCRV &

NAMFREL (also part of the stream of information already pre-programmed).

2.6.c.iii. The consistency of ERs could also be ensured by faked ballots in a staged random manual audit. One must recall the gross lack of transparency of the ballot printing process, which provided ample opportunity, as further cited below, to manufacture fake ballots, including the untrustworthy transportation of ballot boxes by F2 Logistics that put into serious question the integrity of the chain of possession and control of such ballot boxes.

2.7. The Sudden, Unprecedented, and Anomalous Deletion of TS Data. The TS data were suddenly and unusually deleted on the last day of transmissions, May 13, 2022, contrary to the historical norm where the TS data were only deleted on the last day for filing election protests.

2.8. Highly Anomalous, Improbable, and Historically-Abnormal Events and Statistics.

2.8.a. The first transmission to the TS registered at 7:08:50 p.m. during the first hour after voting closed on May 9, 2022 and the 20M+ votes received during that first hour are realistically and logistically impossible and, therefore, highly suspicious because:

2.8.a.i. There are nine (9) major tasks that, based on the time and motion studies conducted by the COMELEC before the elections, take about nineteen (19) minutes minimum time to complete before the VCMs can properly transmit ERs.

2.8.a.ii. Among the tasks referred to in paragraph 2.9.a.i above is the printing of eight (8) copies of ERs for the various poll watchers and candidate representatives, which takes about eight (8) minutes to complete.

2.8.b. Twenty-eight percent (28%) increase in voter registration, compared with the past 50 years wherein the average increase was only three percent (3%)

2.8.c. Constant vote ratio for all presidential & vice-presidential candidates

2.8.d. Constant ratio of actual voters to registered voters of eighty-four to eighty-five percent (84% - 85%) during the first two hours of ER transmissions from all voting precincts in the Philippines, including overseas.

2.8.e. A constant ratio between actual voters to registered voters in overseas voting precincts: In 110 overseas precincts, exactly 1,000 voters out of the 1,000 registered voters voted; in thirty-six (36) overseas precincts, exactly 999 out of the 1,000 registered voters voted.

2.8.f. The peak of ER transmissions abnormally and anomalously occurred during the first hour after voting closed when 317,512 VCMs or 37% of all VCMs transmitted ERs.

2.9.f.i. The TS showed a historically abnormal downturn of only 25,784 VCMs having transmitted during the second hour after voting closed, which is anomalous considering that the peak number of transmissions historically occurs during the second hour.

2.9.f.i. In connection with paragraph 2.9.e.i above, the COMELEC showed in a public presentation after the elections that the peak occurred during the second hour, which contradicted what the TS showed on election night (where the peak occurred during the first hour).

2.8.g. An average of ninety percent (90%) of all ERs transmitted in the vote-rich NCR, Cavite, Batangas, and Laguna region came from single private IP address 192.168.0.2, while the rest came from a few private IP addresses belonging to the 10.x.x. range and an unidentified source.

2.8.h. Out of the 10,462 VCMs in the NCR area, nine private IP addresses transmitted ERs—98.94% of which came from private IP Address 192.168.0.2.

3. OPPORTUNITY to commit electoral fraud.

The COMELEC, Smartmatic (probably in conjunction with the Telcos Globe, Smart, and Dito), F2 Logistics, and the Marcos-Duterte ticket had ample opportunity to preprogram and systematically rig the 2022 Philippine elections to favor a Marcos-Duterte "win."

3.1. COMELEC's Unlawful Practice of Secrecy Provided It With Maximum Opportunity to Commit Electoral Fraud. That the COMELEC now admits—after more than a year of the 2022 NLE and only after the TNTrio had exposed many anomalies in the 2022 NLE and after many unanswered public pleas for the COMELEC to explain such anomalies—to having utilized a wholly private network that used only a few private IP addresses is proof of the COMELEC's unlawful practice of secrecy and clandestine workings that provided it with ample opportunity to commit electoral fraud.

3.1.a. Such secrecy violates the transparency and audibility provisions of Republic Act 9369 and COMELEC Resolution No. 10754.

3.1.b. COMELEC did not allow the election stakeholders, watchdogs, or anyone outside of COMELEC and Smartmatic to witness its SD Card configuration with Smartmatic.

3.1.c. COMELEC kept a significant part of the ballot printing process secret from election watchdogs.

3.1.d. There occurred a sudden, arbitrary, and unilateral deletion on May 13, 2023 (last day of TS data transmissions) of the TS data from journalists' laptops—without due notice of, and the consent, of the journalists and without explanation whatsoever from the COMELEC or the PPCRV, who demanded that journalists surrender their laptops to them before leaving the TS premises and, thus, at this point, appeared to be complicit with the COMELEC.

3.2.d.i. The confiscation and deletion of data from the journalists' laptops is unlawful because it is tantamount to stealing property in the form of previously-stored data and information in the journalists' laptops, the coerced surrender to the PPCRV of which constituted another offense consisting of the unlawful seizure of personal property, and likewise violates Executive Order No. 2 (Freedom of Information) of 2016. (Note: The data or information in the journalists' laptops couldn't be considered exceptions under the law because such information related directly to the elections data, which can never be considered confidential information.)

3.1.e. COMELEC's consistent pattern of behavior of either not being responsive at all to requests for information and documents or extremely delaying to respond to requests for information and documents created for itself ample opportunity to manufacture documents to hide and/or offer an explanation, albeit insufficiently, about what truly happened during the 2022 NLE and how the AES truly worked.

3.1.e.i. COMELEC's public revelation about the Telco Exchange—only after one (1) year and four (4) months had passed since the 2022 NLE—is, by itself, proof of its defense manufacturing and masking of the truth.

3.1.e.ii. It must be emphasized that paragraph 3.2.e.i above, notwithstanding, the Telco Exchange is an incomplete and, thus, lame, attempt to explain and justify the use of illegal private IP addresses in ER transmissions, for in offering the Telco Exchange as a defense to the illegal use of private IP addresses, the COMELEC thereby likewise admitted not only to using a completely different AES compared with the Protocol it had presented to the public before the elections, but that such Telco Exchange is also, from the flimsy way that Chair Garcia described its workings, in clear and gross violation of both election law and the SETS Contract.

3.2. The Nature of AES Technology Allows Multiple Opportunities to Commit Electoral Fraud. By the very nature of the AES technology, there are many various opportunities to feed it with unauthorized or unlawful information or to tamper with it for the purpose of committing electoral fraud, including the following times, among others:

3.2.a. During the manufacture of the VCMs

3.2.b. During the transit or transportation of the VCMs

3.2.c. During the storage of the VCMs in any facility

3.2.d. During the many VCM breakdowns on election day, which constituted eighty (80%) percent of the problems due to VCMs on election day

3.2.e. During the configuration of the SD Cards, which no one outside of COMELEC and Smartmatic had witnessed because COMELEC kept such process secret—again, in violation of Republic Act 9369 and COMELEC Resolution No. 10754.

3.2.f. During the secret ballot printing and processing (in this connection, recall reports of secret "ballot shading" sessions)

@followers
#PunlaParaSaBayan
#MarcosDuterteSinungaling
#COMELECSinungaling
#NAMFRELSinungaling
#PPCRVSinungaling
#MarcosDuterteBerdugo
#MarcosDuterteTraydorSaBayan
#MarcosDuterteTutaNgChina
#TamaNa
#SobraNa
#LabanNa
#MarcosDuterteItakwil
#MarcosDuterteAlisinNa
#OustMarcosDuterte
#PeoplePowerNa

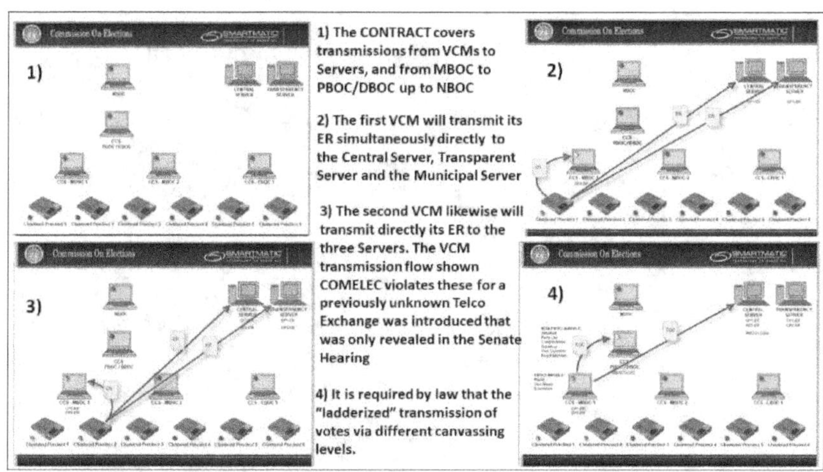

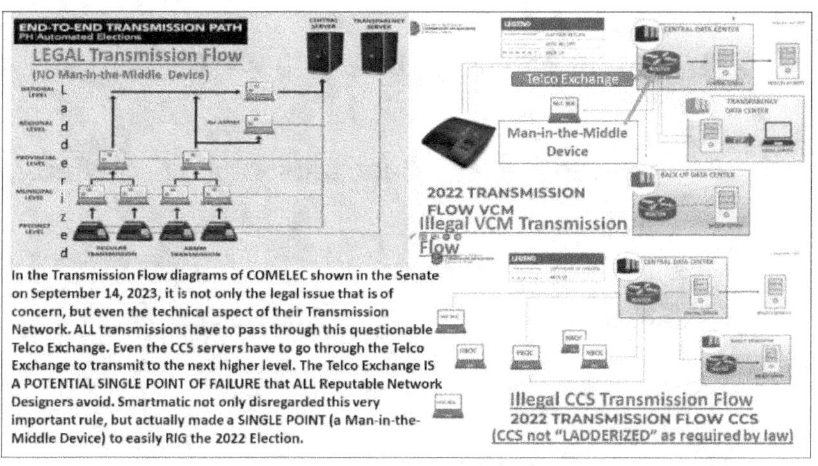

In the Transmission Flow diagrams of COMELEC shown in the Senate on September 14, 2023, it is not only the legal issue that is of concern, but even the technical aspect of their Transmission Network. ALL transmissions have to pass through this questionable Telco Exchange. Even the CCS servers have to go through the Telco Exchange to transmit to the next higher level. The Telco Exchange IS A POTENTIAL SINGLE POINT OF FAILURE that ALL Reputable Network Designers avoid. Smartmatic not only disregarded this very important rule, but actually made a SINGLE POINT (a Man-in-the-Middle Device) to easily RIG the 2022 Election.

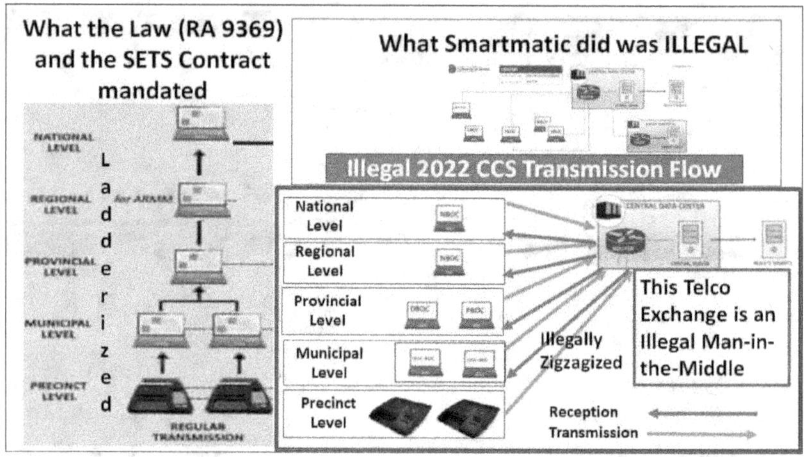

Roman Zarate
Awesome, well done, tuloy ang laban!

Ran Dy
Thanks for the excellent presentation...mabuhay po kayo!

Brgy Asyong
Salamat po!

Edgardo Guardacasa
Brgy Asyong so pano na po? Ano na po gawin? Kung ganyan nagyari?

Brgy Asyong
Edgardo Guardacasa I believe in "the power of the people is greater than the people in power"

Mars L. Dela Cuesta
TRUTH.

....

11
WHO ARE THE TRUE ISRAELITES? – posted at facebook by Felipe Mendoza de Leon is with Tess Campo Olleta.- 2023

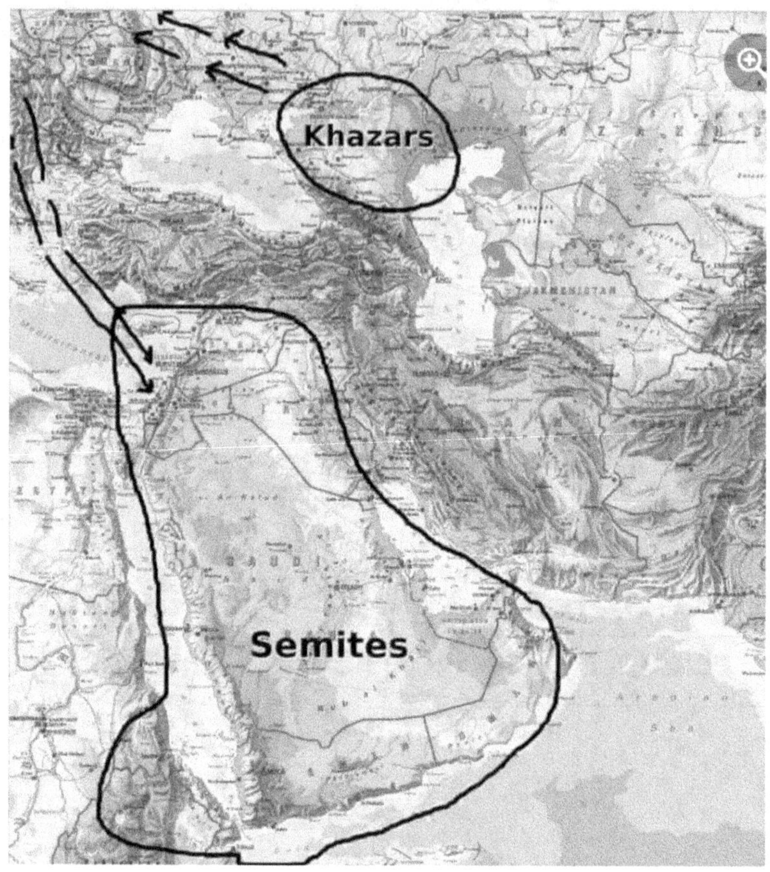

Dr. Areilla Oppenheim at the Hebrew University in Jerusalem, did the first extensive DNA study in 2001 of Israelis & Palestinians, and concluded that the emigrants on ships to Palestine before it became Israel were of Mongol 40% & Turkish 40% genome. There was no Semitic blood associated with the original Hebrews from the Middle East of 4,000 years ago in Jerusalem or Biblical territory.

This was confirmed by another DNA project by Dr. Eran Elhaik at the McKusick-Namans Institute of Genetic Medicine at the John Hopkins University of School of Medicine, in 2012. His conclusions were the same!*

The Askenazi so-called Jews did not ever migrate out of the Middle East!*

At the same time extensive DNA evidence found the Palestinians to have 80% more or less Semitic blood from their ancestors, who were found therefore "to be the real Israelites.

The white Jews whose ancestors embarked on ships in 1882 to Palestine before it was named Israel---aren't Israelites. Truth hurts* once again. These White Eastern European descendants of German, Russian, Polish, Austrian, Georgian, etc., are impostors claiming to be God's Chosen Ones are actually descendants of the old Khazars from the Khazarian Caucasians but they have been denying this scientific evidence as they have made up myths of their own, deluding many Americans for a century now, especially those believing in the Schofield Bible.

The real history of the new established "Israel in 1947" is no secret today!*

Since Palestinians were found to be almost more or at least 80%Semitic. The So-called "chosen people" are on the wrong side of history.

....

12
About Cancer - Sonny Mirasol – Nov. 20, 2023

Copied from a General Chat
and posted for everyone to know
how NOT TO DIE from cancer!

Please share.... If you care 🩶

Hot foods such as curry, chili, and ginger make the body's cancerous cells sleep more* In an international seminar, Dr. Dai, currently at the American Cancer Center, shared his research results on the growth kinetics of cancer cells with the topic "Is Cancer

Curable?" * Cancer is the most exciting The fear is metastasis (transfer).*

Primary cancer does not cause the patient to die, but once the cancer has metastasized, the disturbance in other tissues and organs will cause the patient to die gradually (or quickly). But why some patients whose cancer cells have metastasized have not continued to deteriorate?

Japan has dissected and studied dozens of 90-103-year-olds who passed away naturally without pain, and found that each of them had many cancer cells in their bodies. But why their cancer cells did not cause physical pain? Dr. Dai and several cancer research scholars discovered that cancer cells enter a "dormant period" after being active for a period of time, and then become active again after a period of dormancy, making trouble. The longer the "sleep period", the longer the patient can survive, without even the fearful "metastasis."

The medical community is now actively studying ways to delay the "dormant period" of cancer cells, including the use of drugs and diet. The paper "Effectively Prevent Cell Carcinogenesis" mentioned several natural substances. By controlling the signal transmission in cancer cells, the pathway of (Signal Transduction) allows cancer cells to enter the dormant phase. Please eat more and contain these effective Ingredients of food make the cancer cells in the body sleep more.

1. Curry (the anti-cancer ingredient is curcumin)
2. Pepper (the anti-cancer ingredient is capsaicin)
3. Ginger (the anti-cancer ingredient is curcumin)
4. Green tea (anti-cancer ingredient is catechin)
5. Soy (the anti-cancer ingredient is isoflavones)
6. Tomato (anti-cancer ingredient is lycopene)
7. Grapes (the anti-cancer ingredient is resveratrol)
8. Garlic (the anti-cancer ingredient is sulfide)
9. Cabbage (anti-cancer ingredient is Indole)

10. Cauliflower (the anti-cancer ingredient is sulfide) A pharmacist adds as follows:

This article is passed to everyone, easy to understand.

Because of the recently published longevity drugs Contains the following four: Curcumin/Resveratrol/Silymarin/Astragalus (four ingredients), the first two appear above, mentioned above: curry and ginger are the main anti-cancer ingredients of "curcumin".

The strongest food for detoxification completed by the Academia Sinica for 10 years...in order

1. sweet potatoes
2. Mung beans
3. Oats
4. Pearl Barley
5. Millet
6. Brown rice
7. Red beans
8. Carrots
9. Yam
10. Burdock
11. Asparagus
12. Onions
13. Lotus Root
14. White radish
15. Chrysanthemum vulgaris (Chrysanthemum vulgaris)
16. Sweet potato leaves
17. Turnip leaves
18. Chuanqi
19. Yogurt
20. Vinegar

Remember to save, and please forward it to your friends and family.

....

13
A Moving Story shared by Rafael Evangelista – Nov. 21, 2023 (his 83rdbirthday)

A friend sent me this to read so I thought I'd share it with you. The post brought tears to my eyes. For those of you who know me know that I seldom cry. This is one of those times. God bless! -

Read THE entire thing and warm someone's heart today and pass this along. It's a precious story, just have the tissues ready.

As she stood in front of her 5th grade class on the very first day of school, she told the children an untruth. Like most teachers, she looked at her students and said that she loved them all the same. However, that was impossible, because there in the front row, slumped in his seat, was a little boy named Teddy Stoddard.

Mrs. Thompson had watched Teddy the year before and noticed that he did not play well with the other children, that his clothes were messy and that he constantly needed a bath. In addition, Teddy could be unpleasant.

It got to the point where Mrs. Thompson would actually take delight in marking his papers with a broad red pen, making bold X's and then putting a big "F" at the top of his papers.

At the school where Mrs. Thompson taught, she was required to review each child's past records and she put Teddy's off until last.

However, when she reviewed his file, she was in for a surprise.

Teddy's first grade teacher wrote, "Teddy is a bright child with a ready laugh. He does his work neatly and has good manners... he is a joy to be around.."

His second grade teacher wrote, "Teddy is an excellent student, well liked by his classmates, but he is troubled because his mother has a terminal illness and life at home must be a struggle."

His third grade teacher wrote, "His mother's death has been hard on him. He tries to do his best, but his father doesn't show much interest and his home life will soon affect him if some steps aren't taken."

Teddy's fourth grade teacher wrote, "Teddy is withdrawn and doesn't show much interest in school. He doesn't have many friends and he sometimes sleeps in class."

By now, Mrs. Thompson realized the problem and she was ashamed of herself. She felt even worse when her students brought her Christmas presents, wrapped in beautiful ribbons and bright paper, except for Teddy's. His present was clumsily wrapped in the heavy, brown paper That he got from a grocery bag Mrs. Thompson took pains to open it in the middle of the other presents.

Some of the children started to laugh when she found a rhinestone bracelet with some of the stones missing, and a bottle that was one-quarter full of perfume.. But she stifled the children's laughter when she exclaimed how pretty the bracelet was, putting it on, and dabbing some of the perfume on her wrist.

Teddy Stoddard stayed after school that day just long enough to say, "Mrs. Thompson, today you smelled just like my Mom used to." After the children left, she cried for at least an hour. On that very day, she quit teaching reading, writing and arithmetic. Instead, she began to teach children.

Mrs. Thompson paid particular attention to Teddy. As she worked with him, his mind seemed to come alive. The more she encouraged him, the faster he responded. By the end of the year, Teddy had become one of the smartest children in the class and, despite her lie that she would love all the children the same, Teddy became one of her "teacher's pets.."

A year later, she found a note under her door, from Teddy, telling* her that she was still the best teacher he ever had in his whole life.

Six years went by before she got another note from Teddy. He then wrote that he had finished high school, third in his class, and she was still the best teacher he ever had in life.

Four years after that, she got another letter, saying that while things had been tough at times, he'd stayed in school, had stuck with it, and would soon graduate from college with the highest of honors. He assured Mrs. Thompson that she was still the best and favorite teacher he had ever had in his whole life.

Then four more years passed and yet another letter came. This time he explained that after he got his bachelor's degree, he decided to go a little further. The letter explained that she was still the best and favorite teacher he ever had. But now his name was a little longer.... The letter was signed, Theodore F. Stoddard, MD.

The story does not end there. You see, there was yet another letter that spring. Teddy said he had met this girl and was going to be married. He explained that his father had died a couple of years ago and he was wondering if Mrs. Thompson might agree to sit at the wedding in the place that was usually reserved for the mother of the groom.

Of course, Mrs. Thompson did. And guess what? She wore that bracelet, the one with several rhinestones missing. Moreover, she made sure she was wearing the perfume that Teddy remembered his mother wearing on their last Christmas together.

They hugged each other, and Dr. Stoddard whispered in Mrs. Thompson's ear, "Thank you Mrs. Thompson for* believing in me. Thank you so much for making me feel important and showing me that I could make a difference."

Mrs. Thompson, with tears in her eyes, whispered back. She said, "Teddy, you have it all wrong. You were the one who taught me that I could make a difference. I didn't know how to teach until I met you."

(For you that don't know, Teddy Stoddard is the Dr. at Iowa Methodist Hospital in Des Moines that has the Stoddard Cancer Wing.)

Just try to make a difference in someone's life today? tomorrow? Just "do it".

Random acts of kindness, I think they call it?

"Believe in Angels, then return the favor."

Credits: Unknown

....

14
CLARIFICATORY STATEMENT TO HELP FRANK YSAAC AND SOME OF HIS AND THE TNTRIO's FOLLOWERS FOCUS ON THE REAL ISSUES—NOT ME – Victoria Smith – Nov. 20, 2023

I. THE FACTS:

Last week, Frank Ysaac of TNTrio announced TNTrio's acceptance of COMELEC's offer to settle the issues TNTrio raised about the 2022 NLE by opening the ballot boxes and conducting a recount. Ysaac attached a photo of TNTrio's letter of acceptance, which showed that it asked for no condition (not even for details of how such recount would be conducted or the consequences of such a process), except that COMELEC issue an en banc resolution on the matter.

I commented to that post, stating I failed to fathom why TNTrio agreed to this, despite TNTrio itself having proven COMELEC deceptive.

Ysaac replied by saying we should simply trust him and the TNTrio. I responded with a rejoinder that, due to the substantial amounts donated by the Filipino people to TNTrio to help it pay for its legal fees and expenses (which I then estimated at ranging between Php1.5 - 2M), TNTrio has a responsibility to be accountable to the people for its decisions and actions.

How did Ysaac react? He blocked me from his page and posted libelous statements against me—among others, calling me a "detractor" and a "liar." In addition, he repeatedly described me as someone "based abroad," suggesting that I and all my fellow expatriate Filipinos are less patriotic than Filipinos in the Philippines and, therefore, unworthy of speaking out on the issues and challenging TNTrio.

By his words and actions toward me, Ysaac demonstrated ignorance or dismissiveness of, and ungratefulness for my many courageous and passionate advocacy posts, presentations, projects, and personal sacrifices to which many other Filipinos have attested, including his TNTRio partner, General Eliseo Rio, Jr., as having helped and supported not only the TNTrio but the Filipino people's ultimate fight to restore truth, democracy, and justice in the Philippines.

Moreover, by his inflammatory statements, Ysaac incited his followers to treat me with contempt and launch a smear campaign against me. This is shown by his followers following his lead exactly: issuing similar libelous statements against me and blocking me from replying to their false statements about me in their pages—where they posted such libelous statements—thereby denying me my human and legal right to defend myself and promoting and propagating false beliefs about me aimed at casting aspersions on my personal integrity.

Meanwhile, Ysaac, TNTrio, and their followers failed and continue to fail to answer my just and valid questions. Thus, THE REAL ISSUES REMAIN UNANSWERED.

Therefore, I am forced to issue this statement to set the record straight and defend my good name, which is one of the few things of real value to me—for I have no ambition to run for public office or to be famous, contrary to what some misguided TNTrio followers accuse me of. I'm only motivated by true love of country and people.

I hope the following could help Ysaac and his followers to refocus their attention on the real issues:

1. I gave an estimate—an estimate that wasn't meant to be an accurate accounting or absolute declaration of the exact amount TNTrio has paid their lawyers or the amounts donated to them to help defray their legal expenses.

2. The estimate was based on my knowledge of financial statements and documents that show that for the months of April to July 2023, TNTrio's lawyers billed an average monthly retainer fee of US$2,100. This was only for the Mandamus Petition—which has now reached its first anniversary—with no success.

Based on an exchange rate of Php 55 to US$1, I multiplied US$2,100 by twelve (12) months and roughly estimated the total to be equivalent to Php 1.5M, which was not far from the accurate calculation of the sum of Php 1.386M.

3. At the time I became privy to such financial statements, I was new to the organization that had helped TNTrio raise funds to pay their lawyers. I soon left that organization because I felt I could be a more effective advocate outside such organization.

4. Considering that TNTrio had since initiated two other cases with the help of their lawyers (the move to impeach COMELEC Commissioners and the Petition to Disqualify Smartmatic), I reasonably assumed such cases generated more lawyer's fees and other legal expenses.

Thus, it is no wonder why TNTrio and their supporters continue to plead with the Filipino people for additional financial support.

5. I made a rough estimate of TNTrio's total legal expenses to-date by multiplying my estimate of Php 1.5 by three (the 3 cases), which gave me about Php 4.5M. But since the two new cases had only been pending for a few months, I thought it reasonable to simply divide the rounded figure of Php 4M by half to arrive at a rough total estimate of Php 2M.

6. While my estimate may be inaccurate (which is, after all, what an estimate is), the estimated amounts were NOT the point of my comments to Ysaac and his followers.

II. THE (TRUE) ISSUE:

My point, which Ysaac and his followers failed and continue to fail to properly address (perhaps because by trying to attack my credibility they hope to escape answering my valid questions), was this:

TNTrio, by asking for and receiving the Filipino people's support, financial and moral, for their actions, thereby held themselves accountable to the people for their actions and decisions—such as explaining why they agreed, practically unconditionally, to accept COMELEC's overeager offer to open ballot boxes despite the TNTrio itself having countlessly proven COMELEC to be consistently deceptive.

THAT was the issue I raised. Was it wrong for me to raise it? Absolutely not.

Ysaac claims only about Php 400,00 had been billed by or paid to the TNTrio's lawyers. Does this make it any less the TNTrio's obligation to the Filipino people to account for their decisions and actions, allegedly on advice of their lawyers, especially if such decisions and actions defy logic?

No one should be immune to critique or questioning—not even the TNTrio, for that would make them dictators and hypocrites.

When they asked for, and received the Filipino people's support, they ceased to possess the prerogative of private citizens in having the exclusive say on their decisions and actions—for they thereby ceased to be merely private citizens but public servants to all of us.

And they should have at least respected and listened to their fellow advocates' opinions on how to pursue the advocacy we now all share. That's what true leaders do.

III. CONCLUSION:

By Ysaac and his followers attacking me personally, they attempted to silence me on an important issue. They chose to deflect blame for their failure to answer my just and valid questions by distracting the public through ad hominem attacks against my personal integrity.

Therefore, they, not me, are the true detractors. They, not me, are the ones who render themselves guilty of libel—against me. They, not me, are the ones hiding the truth by their refusal to answer my fair and valid questions.

May truth prevail, for only the turn could set our people free.

The question now is: Would Ysaac, along with his partners in TNTrio and their followers, now choose to be true to the "truth" and transparency" in the TNTrio name?

Rico Cadayona

Naging sensitive para sa kanila ang iyong question dahil sa question about how much was paid to the lawyers. This a two part valid questions: 1. Why did TNTrio agree to the opening of the ballot considering all circumstances surrounding the issue. 2. How much was actually paid to the lawyers. A third question should have been : where is the accounting?

The money question part is the one that triggered them to be mad and started attacking you. This is speculation on my part, but I can bet my 2 cents, I'm correct. The lawyers fees should have been devulged upfront. Its ok to pay the lawyers but TNTrio is obligated to report how much was collected and how much was paid. Fund raising yun eh. Yung question mo about the money is what they set them on fire.

They tried to do the same thing to me when I started to be critical of FYs prophecies without miracles. Two of TNTrio supporters scolded me to stop being negative. Wala daw naman ginagawa para makatulong sa TNTrio. Puro dakdak lang daw tayo sa socmed. Pinatahimik ko sila agad. Ipinakita ko sa kanila ang RESIBO ng mga contributions ko so far sa TNtrio. I will not mention the amount here. But its not peanuts. TThen I told them that you , Atty Victoria Smith can barely afford a good 2 hour continous sleep thinking and working day in day out on how to help and makec a differenc Then I ask the treasurer for accounting detailed accounting kung ano ang nangyari sa collected funds including those collected from others_ abroad and locally.so far all I got some sketchy report, hindi accounting, and a thank you note. Tumahimik sila . Obviously they were not aware of my contributions THen they asked me to just help the cause and stop ' making noises"and "rocking the boat". Im still waiting for their apologies.I think maraming ahas sa loob ng TNTrio. Mabababa ang pagkatao at sarado ang isip..PALAGAY KO may mga personal agenda. Sayang naniniwala pa naman ako sa findings ng TNTrio. I hope hindi ito masayang.

So just be very careful.

Aurora Ramos
Rico Cadayona Rico Cadayona Why did the advocacy turn sour? Are there indi ideals out to discredit the integrity and the sdvocacy of the TNTRIO ? With the

way things are going , it is probable that the support from the patriotic donors will weaken. The fake leaders will be so happy with the turn of events on our side. That's a very sad news on the improvement of the cases that are being pursued . The enemies are laughing their heart out because they are winning th battle through delaying tactics that woud drain our resures until we suddenly stop for lack of funds to pay the pfs of the lawyers hired. So disgusting why it has to come to this comotion !

Aurora Ramos
Correction:individuals not ideals, advocacy, the battle not th, would drain not would, resources not resurces

Yvad Onauo
In order this issue won't get too chaotic, both parties should stop besmirching. This won't bring good to our crusade.

I understand darn well Atty Victoria's concern on TNTrio's acceptance on COMELEC's offer for ballot counting. Should have been more specific on how it's done. Her questions are valid including TNTrio's financial accountability since it originates from public fund raising.

Since TNTrio is personally engaging with the case with their lawyer, let's just wish them all the best to succeed.

Sonny Mirasol
Yvad Onauo is it not only one party doing the besmirching?

And if both are doing it as you say, did not that party do it first?

....

15

Screams from Gaza – Zeina Assma – posted by Rhess Encinas at FB – Nov. 22, 2023

Write my name on my leg, Mama
Use the black permanent marker
with the ink that doesn't bleed
if it gets wet, the one that doesn't melt
if it's exposed to heat

Write my name on my leg, Mama
Make the lines thick and clear
Add your special flourishes
so I can take comfort in seeing
my mama's handwriting when I go to sleep

Write my name on my leg, Mama
and on the legs of my sisters and brothers
This way we will belong together
This way we will be known
as your children

Write my name on my leg, Mama
and please write your name
and Baba's name on your legs, too
so we will be remembered
as a family

Write my name on my leg, Mama
Don't add any numbers
like when I was born or the address of our home
I don't want the world to list me as a number
I have a name and I am not a number

Write my name on my leg, Mama
When the bomb hits our house
When the walls crush our skulls and bones

our legs will tell our story, how
there was nowhere for us to run
—Zeina Azzam

"SCREAM FROM GAZA" by Artist Omar Esstar

....

16
Essay – Story of Slavery – Ronnie Hopson – Alabama – Nov. 2023

A1 - When Did Slavery Start?

Hundreds of thousands of Africans, both free and enslaved, aided the establishment and survival of colonies in the Americas and the New World. However, many consider a significant starting point to slavery in America to be 1619, when the privateer The White Lion brought 20 enslaved African ashore in the British colony of Jamestown, Virginia. The crew had seized the Africans from the Portuguese slave ship Sao Jao Bautista.

Throughout the 17th century, European settlers in

North America turned to enslaved Africans as a cheaper, more plentiful labor source than indentured servants, who were mostly poor Europeans.

Though it is impossible to give accurate figures, I estimate that 6 to 7 million enslaved people were imported to the New World during the 18th century alone, depriving the African continent of some of its healthiest and ablest men and women. How can a generation recover with these losses?

In the 17th and 18th centuries, enslaved Africans worked mainly on the tobacco, rice and indigo plantations of the southern coast, from the Chesapeake Bay colonies of Maryland and Virginia south to Georgia.

After the American Revolution, many colonists—particularly in the North, where slavery was relatively unimportant to the agricultural economy—began to link the oppression of enslaved Africans to their own oppression by the British, and to call for slavery's abolition. A change was on the way....

But after the Revolutionary War, the new U.S. Constitution tacitly acknowledged the institution of slavery, counting each enslaved individual as three-fifths of a person for the purposes of taxation and representation in Congress and guaranteeing the right to repossess any "person held to service or labor" (an obvious euphemism for slavery).

Slavery itself was never widespread in the North, though many of the region's businessmen grew rich on the slave trade and investments in southern plantations.

They still are!!! Between 1774 and 1804, most of the northern states abolished slavery or started the process to abolish slavery, but the institution of slavery remained vital to the South. Mentally, we are still very much there....

Though the U.S. Congress outlawed the African slave trade in 1808, the domestic trade flourished, and the enslaved population in the United States nearly tripled overthe next 50 years. By 1860 it had reached nearly 4 million, with more than half living in the cotton-producing states of the South.

A2 - History of Slavery

Enslaved people in the antebellum South constituted about one-third of the southern population. Most lived on large plantations or small farms; many masters owned fewer than 50 enslaved people.

Landowners sought to make their enslaved completely dependent on them through a system of restrictive codes. They were usually prohibited from learning to read and write, and their behavior and movement were restricted. My people were insulted daily and no one cared....

Many masters raped enslaved women, and rewarded obedient behavior with favors, while rebellious enslaved people were brutally punished. A strict hierarchy among the enslaved (from privileged house workers and skilled artisans down to lowly field hands) helped keep them divided and less likely to organize against their masters.

Marriages between enslaved men and women had no legal basis, but many did marry and raise large families; most owners of enslaved workers encouraged this practice, but nonetheless did not usually hesitate to divide families by sale or removal.

A3 - Slave Rebellions

Rebellions among enslaved people did occur—notably, ones led by Gabriel Prosser in Richmond in 1800 and by Denmark Vesey in Charleston in 1822—but few were successful.

The revolt that most terrified enslavers was that led by Nat Turner in Southampton County, Virginia, in August 1831. Turner's group, which eventually numbered around 75 Black men, murdered some 55-white people in two days before armed resistance from local white people and the arrival of state militia forces overwhelmed them.

Supporters of slavery pointed to Turner's rebellion

as evidence that Black people were inherently inferior barbarians requiring an institution such as slavery to discipline them, and fears of similar insurrections led many southern states to further strengthen their slave codes in order to limit the education, movement and assembly of enslaved people. The shock of it all...

A4 - Abolitionist Movement

In the North, the increased repression of southern Black people only fanned the flames of the growing abolitionist movement.

From the 1830s to the 1860s, the movement to abolish slavery in America gained strength, led by free Black people such as Frederick Douglass and white supporters such as William Lloyd Garrison, founder of the radical newspaper The Liberator, and Harriet Beecher Stowe, who published the bestselling antislavery novel Under Tom's Cabin.

While many abolitionists based their activism on the belief that slaveholding was a sin, others were more inclined to the non-religious "free-labor" argument, which held that slaveholding was regressive, inefficient and made little economic sense.

Free Black people and other antislavery northerners had begun helping enslaved people escape from southern plantations to the North via a loose network of safe houses as early as the 1780s. This practice, known as the Underground Railroad, gained real momentum in the 1830s. Conductors like Harriet Tubman guided escapees on their journey North, and "stationmasters" included such prominent figures as Frederick Douglass, Secretary of State William H. Seward and Pennsylvania congressman Thaddeus Stevens. Although estimates vary widely, it may have helped anywhere from 40,000 to 100,000 enslaved people reach freedom.

The success of the Underground Railroad helped spread abolitionist feelings in the North; it also undoubtedly increased sectional tensions, convincing pro-slavery southerners of their northern countrymen's determination to defeat the institution that sustained them.

A5 - Civil War

The South would reach the breaking point the following year, when Republican candidate Lincoln was elected as president. Within three months, seven southern states had seceded to form the Confederate States of America; four more would follow after the Civil War began. Though Lincoln's anti-slavery views were well
established, the central Union war aim at first was not to abolish slavery, but to preserve the United States as a nation.

Abolition became a goal only later, due to military necessity, growing anti-slavery sentiment in the North and the self-emancipation of many people who fled enslavement as Union troops swept through the South.

A6 - When Did Slavery End?

On September 22,1862, Lincoln issued a preliminary emancipation proclamation, and on January 1,1863, he made it official that "slaves within any State, or

designated part of a State...in rebellion,...shall be then, thenceforward, and forever free."

By freeing some 3 million enslaved people in the rebel states, the Emancipation Proclamation deprived the Confederacy of the bulk of its labor forces and put international public opinion strongly on the Union side.

Though the Emancipation Proclamation didn't officially end all slavery in America—that would happen with the passage of the 13th Amendment after the Civil War's end in 1865—some 186,000 Black soldiers would join the Union Army, and about 38,000 lost their lives.

The 13th Amendment, adopted on December 18, 1865, officially abolished slavery, but freed Black peoples' status in the post-war South remained precarious, and

significant challenges awaited during the Reconstruction period.

Previously enslaved men and women received the rights of citizenship and the "equal protection" of the Constitution in the Amendment and the right to vote in the 15th Amendment, but these provisions of the Constitution were often ignored or violated, and it was difficult for Black citizens to gain a foothold in the post-war economy thanks to restrictive Black codes and regressive contractual arrangements suchas sharecropping. The more things change, the more they stay same...

Despite seeing an unprecedented degree of Black participation in American political life, Reconstruction was ultimately frustrating for African Americans, and the rebirth of white supremacy—including the rise of racist organizations such as the Ku Klux Klan (KKK)—had triumphed in the South by 1877.

Almost a century later, resistance to the lingering racism and discrimination in America that began during the slavery era led to the civil rights movement of the 1960s, which achieved the greatest political and social gains for Black Americans since Reconstruction.

A7 - What We are Owed!

The trans-Atlantic slave-trade was the capture, forcible transport and sale of native Africans to Europeans for lifelong bondage in the Americas. Lasting from the 16th to 19th centuries, it is responsible, more than any other project or phenomenon in the history of the modern world, for the creation of the African diaspora—the dispersal of Black people outside their places of origin on the continent of Africa.

As a result of the trans-Atlantic slave trade, there are presently 51.5 million people of African descent living in North America (United States, Mexico, and Canada), approximately 66 million in South America, 1.9 million in Central America, and more than 14.5 million throughout the islands of the Caribbean. Over centuries of transformation and upheaval, these diasporic peoples have developed rich cultural traditions, distinct societies and independent nations—all sharing elements of a common African heritage.

The trans-Atlantic slave trade was one leg of a three-part system known as the triangular trade. The forming of the triangle began when European ships, carrying and firearms and manufactured goods, sailed to Africa, where the commodities were traded for enslaved men, women and children. Next, the same ships transported the human cargo across the Atlantic Ocean to the Americas.

This horrific journey was called the Middle Passage. Completing the triangle, the ships—having disembarked the enslaved Africans—were reloaded with cotton, sugar, tobacco and other cash crops produced by slave labor, and returned to Europe.

The triangular trade generated incredible wealth for the European and American nations that participated in it—at the expense of millions of human lives. An estimated 1.8 million Africans perished during the Middle Passage.

The countries that enslaved the highest number of Africans, from the most to the least, were Portugal, Britain, France, the Netherlands, Spain, the United States and Denmark—shipping a total of 12.5 million enslaved Africans to toil in what was considered the "New World."

A8 - Trade

Another downplayed factor is the central role played by ruling African states in the capture and sale of fellow Africans to European traders—an estimated 90 percent of all captives. The main motivation behind these transactions was the acquisition of guns for use in inter-ethnic warfare. The enslaved were abducted from as far north as present-day Senegal to as far south as Angola and transported to destinations as far south as Argentina and as far north as New England.

Dehumanizing in all locations, the practice of slavery still could vary from place to place. This variation accounts for demographic, cultural and even genetic distinctions among modern diasporic Black populations.

History shows that enslaved women contributed more than enslaved men to themodern-day gene pool of people of African descent in the Americas. The findings also show that Caucasian men contributed more than Caucasian women, confirming the well-documented practice of sexual violation of enslaved women. We knew this, but it needs to be said. For the nearly four centuries before its abolition by all nations involved, "the trans-Atlantic slave trade not only influenced the composition of slave communities in the Americas, it also powerfully shaped slave resistance.

A9 - From Me to You (About the Author of Essay)

President John F. Kennedy once said, "Ask not what your country can do for you. Ask what you can do for your country"!

My name is **Ronnie Hopson, Sr.** I am the Founder and CEO of Foundation for Research in Ebony Economics, Inc. We are a small Southern Based 501 (c)(3) Non-Profit Organization. We specialize in permanent solutions to economic, financial and people management problems.

(NOTE: The above essay will be converted into a separate book, including Ronnie Hopson poems. His book will hopefully come out in 2024.-Tatay Jobo)

....

17
The sorbetero of Roselle. IL. makes an expatriate nostalgic - Fred Natividad, Berwyn, Illinois

– 1996

Chicago Magazine, in its issue of July. 2001, featured on page 146 a Filipino "sorbetero" (ice cream vendor). The sorbetero, complete with a home-painted pushcart commonly seen in the Philippines - commonly seen in my time, at least - was part of the Filipino motif of the Bahay Kubo, a Philippine-American restaurant in suburban Roselle, Illinois. The Bahay Kubo was the subject of a review by Joanne Treslrail in the glossy magazine's restaurant pages.

The sorbetero evoked memories...

...Another sorbetero in the rural town of Tolong who pushed his cart on the dusty streets while he rang a hand-held bell to announce his presence...

When I was growing up in Tolong somewhere in the Philippines (and I am now a 68-ycar old expatriate in the Chicago area) I was quite familiar with the town sorbetero because he was from my neighborhood called Lumbaan. A less stony part of Tolong. Lumbaan was (probably still is) very low in the eyes of idiotic elitists/snobs. Some character once libeled us by calling our neighborhood a haven of thieves.

Not that this church-going character could claim honesty as an outstanding virtue himself... but that's another story... Just believe me that even in a miserable little town like Tolong, there are elitists/snobs and they arc. without being conscious of it, hilarious because of their brazen hypocrisy.

Like most of us in the neighborhood, he was very, very poor. But he did not steal pigs to survive. He sold home-made ice cream, which, naturally, was not the best in the world. After all he was not a wealthy capitalist like the Manila makers of Magnolia Icc Cream who could afford better ingredients.

Still, to children all over our little town his cheap stuff was a novelty - ice cream was always a novelty. 1

didn't realize it then but, of course, the torrid Philippine climate had something to do with the popularity of anything cold. In fact the sorbetero's competitor is not another ice-cream vendor but another kind of sidewalk entrepreneur - the halo-halo vendor whose advantage is that halo-halo is a lot simpler to make. Just cut up pieces of fruit and layer them m a glass, add shaved ice, sugar and a tablespoon of canned evaporated milk. Bingo, you have halo-halo. And, like ice cream, its selling point is that it is cold because its main ingredient is simply a tiny piece of ice that expanded in volume when it was manhandled with a scraping tool to convert it to snowlike shaved ice.

Our sorbetero's business advantage over the halo-halo vendor is that he, the sorbetero, is mobile He would push his cart all over tow n and his favorite spot was in front of the schoolyard. He would time his appearance at recess time when children would be all over him clamoring to buy his tiny cones. The dust storms created by the stampede of bare feet certainly contaminated the exposed cones. But who cares?

**Ernesto Juntura, staff of Bahay Kubo
plays Sorbetero In Roselle, IL.**

Sanitation at that time may be well below the standards we demand today but I have a feeling that our immune systems might have been stronger then How else can it be explained why I don't remember any diarrhea epidemic among the sorbetero's clients who slurped his dust-laden ice cream?

'Vhen recess is over and his spot gets eerily deserted he would put out his age-worn bell and starts ringing it as he pushes his cart towards the municipal building where unproductive loafers hang out for want of anything to do. He might sell a few cones there and then he pushes on to the southern part of town - the dilapidated equivalent of a "downtown" - where there arc a few ma-and-pa grocery stores, vegetable stands, a barbershop, a tailor shop...

Fifty years ago I left Tolong for good when I went to college in Manila on my father's educational benefits as a WW II veteran. It must have been at this time when I was last conscious of my neighbor, the sorbetero, because .../ hometown visits were rare and brief. Most likely the education of his children would be just basic reading and writing. Anything higher would be beyond reach unless he won the sweepstakes. There was little hope that his family could have escaped a vicious, permanent cycle of poverty. After all. our neighborhood could very well be a microcosm of national Philippine endemic poverty, where people like the sorbetero are important only during election time but callously ignored afterwards...

Anyway, after fifty years, I remember from out of the blue, my sorbetero neighbor, thanks to a theatrical sorbetero at the Bahay Kubo in Roselle. Illinois. With vividness I remember his stoic will to survive with his scant productivity.

He could be dead now, leading me to wonder whatever happened to his family.

....

18

Where is my America?
By Philip S. Chua

In 1936 when I was born, everyone clearly knew I was a boy and that I was a he, for people then had common sense and cerebral lucidity.

Today, there is a debate about him and her, and he and she, amidst the confusion and fear of when and what to say, where even a US Supreme Court Justice nominee was ignorant of her own gender identity.

Indeed, the destructive vulture of wokeism has infested so many, the radicals with impunity spreading havoc and chaos to society.

And there are revisionist calls for historical monuments to fall, a brainless movement to defund the Police and abolish ICE, an insanity of lawlessness, and selfishness, cancel culture,

Black, White, Muslim, and Asian hate, a prolific demand for infants-not-to-be as barren couples in anxious despair wait, and mutilation of children behind their parents' back.

Racism, sexism, massive abuse of the freedom of speech, injustice from weaponized government hounds, and the quake of national fragmentation in our midst, abridging individual and societal amendment rights, creating a sad, tilted, and dangerous world for all: a broken family, a broken home, a broken America.

The nation's borders purposedly left agape, pregnant with unvetted illegals, more than 10 million crashing in, two million "got-aways":

Cartel's killers, rapists, drug and sex traffickers, child molester and terrorists, who might even now be plotting an Armageddon from within, all this burden on the taxpayers' shoulders and at the nation's peril – robbing citizens of their privacy, resources, security, and peace.

Sanctuary cities now reneging on their promises as painful reality hits.

There is wanton murder of policemen, senseless killings on the streets, mugging of young and old, open destruction and looting of stores and burning flags and properties in various liberal sectors, as justice intentionally looks the other way and continues its slumber in woke and liberal lunacy.

The thunderous chants of misguided, history-anemic, ivy-league students and other seditious ignorant bigots

"Death to America, Death to Israel," the provocative evil cry to annihilate all the Jews to erase Israel and singing praises no less to those barbaric bin Laden monsters who behead babies, rape women, burn people alive, and kill innocent seniors and children, are deafening, evil, gruesome, nauseating.

Can anyone, on any side, think of any justification for these diabolical acts?

Chaos and stupidity grip our nation, as the world quivers over a nuclear end, people confused, scared, and on their knees.

Those who hate America, all the thankless ingrates, vilipenders, should leave our gracious shores, our noble land, and with them take this virus of massive insanity, the pandemic of anger, hatred, and inhumanity.

This madness must stop!

Where is my America of yesteryears, where godliness, respect for law and order, compassion, love of fellowmen, tolerance, and kindness abound, and where integrity and dignity were sacred, sometimes chosen more valuable than life itself?

I miss my America, land of the wise and noble free, during its golden years of greatness, and the wonders of all its tenderhearted souls.

In supplication, gripped by sadness, buoyed by a ray of hope,

I pray for God to wake and shake us all from this repulsive and horrifying nightmare, and bless us all with wisdom, compassion, and care to fulfill our common aspirations and noble dreams as One, for America's best eons yet to come.

Reprinted from MALAYA, PTSN, and PAAN. The author, Philip S. Chua, MD, FACS, FPCS, (BetanHeart '55 - UPD), a Cardiac Surgeon Emeritus based in Northwest Indiana and Las Vegas, Nevada, is a Fellow of the American College of Surgeons, an international medical lecturer/author, medical missionary, health advocate, newspaper columnist, and Chairman of the Filipino United Network-USA, a 501(c)3 humanitarian foundation in the United States. He was a decorated recipient of the Indiana Sagamore of the Wabash Award in 1995, conferred by then Indiana Governor, later Senator, and then presidential candidate, Evan Bayh. Other Sagamore past awardees include President Harry Truman, President George HW Bush, Muhammad Ali, Astronaut Gus Grissom (Wikipedia). Websites: FUN8888.com and philipSchua.com Email: scalpelpen@gmail.com

....

19
Relevant Posters

16 SENATORS WHO VOTED TO OUST DE LIMA
4 SENATORS WHO VOTED AGAINST DE LIMA'S OUSTER
2 ABSTAINED
2 DID NOT VOTE
RAPPLER

THE ROAD NOT TAKEN
Robert Frost

Two roads diverged in a yellow wood,
And sorry I could not travel both
And be one traveler, long I stood
And looked down one as far as I could
To where it bent in the undergrowth;

Then took the other, as just as fair,
And having perhaps the better claim,
Because it was grassy and wanted wear;
Though as for that the passing there
Had worn them really about the same,

And both that morning equally lay
In leaves no step had trodden black.
Oh, I kept the first for another day!
Yet knowing how way leads on to way,
I doubted if I should ever come back.

I shall be telling this with a sigh
Somewhere ages and ages hence:
Two roads diverged in a wood, and I—
I took the one less traveled by,
And that has made all the difference.

. . . .

END